WTO, TRIPS, and Geographical Indications (GIs)

WTO, TRIPS, and Geographical Indications (GIs)

Edited by

Tapan Kumar Rout

Deputy Director, Textiles Committee, Ministry of Textiles, Government of India, Mumbai

and

Bidyadhar Majhi

Joint Director (Economics), Competition Commission of India, Ministry of Corporate Affairs, Government of India, New Delhi

New Century Publications

New Delhi, India

NEW CENTURY PUBLICATIONS
4852 / 24, 1st Floor,
Ansari Road, Daryaganj,
New Delhi – 110 002 (India)

Tel.: 011-4101 7798; 4358 7398; 98112 66355
E-mail: info@newcenturypublications.com

www.newcenturypublications.com

Editorial office:
4800 / 24, Bharat Ram Road,
Ansari Road, Daryaganj,
New Delhi – 110 002

Reprint: 2024

ISBN: **978-81-7708-371-2**

First Published: 2014

Published by New Century Publications and printed at Milan Enterprises, New Delhi.

Designs: Patch Creative Unit, New Delhi.

PRINTED IN INDIA

About the Book

Intellectual property rights (IPRs) refer to the legal ownership by a person or business of an invention/discovery attached to a particular product or process which protects the owner against unauthorized copying or imitation.

The Agreement establishing the World Trade Organization (WTO) contains, *inter alia*, an Agreement on Trade Related Aspects of Intellectual Property Rights (TRIPS). The TRIPS Agreement, which came into effect on January 1, 1995, is till date the most comprehensive multilateral agreement on intellectual property rights. TRIPS provides for norms and standards in respect of following areas of intellectual property: (i) copyright and related rights (i.e. the rights of performers, producers of sound recordings and broadcasting organizations); (ii) trademarks including service marks; (iii) geographical indications including appellations of origin; (iv) industrial designs; (v) patents including the protection of new varieties of plants; (vi) layout designs of integrated circuits; (vii) undisclosed information including trade secrets and test data; and (viii) control of anti-competitive practices in contractual licences.

Geographical indications (GIs) are defined, for the purposes of the Agreement, as indications which identify a good originating in the territory of a Member, or a region or locality in that territory, where a given quality, reputation or other characteristic of the good is essentially attributable to its geographical origin.

This book contains 10 research papers—authored by experts in the field—which explore the socio-economic implications of intellectual property rights protection through geographical indications and analyze the legal aspects associated with the registration of products in the Indian context.

About the Editors

Shri Tapan Kumar Rout is presently Deputy Director in the Textiles Committee, Ministry of Textiles, Government of India, Mumbai. An M.A. in Economics, he is an expert on international trade and globalization. He has to his credit more than 40 research publications. His current research areas include intellectual property rights (IPRs), trade facilitation, and non-tariff barriers (NTBs).

Dr. Bidyadhar Majhi is currently Joint Director (Economics), Competition Commission of India, Ministry of Corporate Affairs, Government of India, New Delhi. Previously, he was a faculty member of Indian Institute of Foreign Trade (IIFT), New Delhi; Shyam Lal College (University of Delhi); Institute of Chartered Accountants of India (ICAI), New Delhi; and Government College, Phulbani, Odisha.

Contents

Contributors

Ramakrushna Panigrahi	Associate Professor of Economics and International Business, International Management Institute (IMI), Bhubaneswar.
Tapan Kumar Rout	Deputy Director, Textiles Committee, Ministry of Textiles, Government of India, Mumbai.
T.N. Singh	Department of Earth Sciences, Indian Institute Technology (IIT), Mumbai.
Anuradha Maheshwari	Director, Institute of Intellectual Property Studies, NMIMS University, Mumbai.
Debdatta Pal	Doctoral Student, Indian Institute of Management (IIM), Ahmedabad.
Amlan Das	Post-graduate from Indian Institute of Management (IIM), Ahmedabad.
Raju K.D.	Assistant Professor, Rajiv Gandhi School of Intellectual Property Law, Indian Institute of Technology (IIT), Kharagpur.
Apoorva Sharma	Rajiv Gandhi School of Intellectual Property Law, Indian Institute of Technology (IIT), Kharagpur.
Shakeel Ahamed	Field Officer, Textiles Committee, Ministry of Textiles, Government of India, Mumbai.
Bidyadhar Majhi	Joint Director (Economics), Competition Commission of India, Ministry of Corporate Affairs, Government of India, New Delhi.
S.K. Soam	Head, Information and Communication Division, National Academy of Agricultural Research Management (NAARM), Hyderabad.

Preface

Intellectual property rights (IPRs) refer to the legal ownership by a person or business of an invention/discovery attached to particular product or process which protects the owner against unauthorized copying or imitation.

The Agreement establishing the World Trade Organization (WTO) contains, *inter alia*, an Agreement on Trade Related Aspects of Intellectual Property Rights (TRIPS). TRIPS Agreement is Annex 1C of the Marrakesh Agreement establishing the World Trade Organization (WTO), signed in Marrakesh, Morocco on April 15, 1994.

The TRIPS Agreement, which came into effect on 1st January 1995, is to date the most comprehensive multilateral agreement on intellectual property.

TRIPS provides for norms and standards in respect of following areas of intellectual property:

1. Copyright and related rights (i.e. the rights of performers, producers of sound recordings and broadcasting organizations).
2. Trademarks including service marks.
3. Geographical indications including appellations of origin.
4. Industrial designs.
5. Patents including the protection of new varieties of plants.
6. Layout-designs of integrated circuits.
7. Undisclosed information including trade secrets and test data.
8. Control of anti-competitive practices in contractual licences.

Geographical indications are defined, for the purposes of the Agreement, as indications which identify a good as originating in the territory of a Member, or a region or locality in that territory, where a given quality, reputation or other characteristic of the good is essentially attributable to its geographical origin (Article 22.1). Thus, this definition specifies that the quality, reputation or other characteristics of a good can each be a sufficient basis for eligibility as a geographical indication, where they are essentially attributable to the geographical origin of the good.

In respect of all geographical indications, interested parties must have legal means to prevent use of indications which mislead the public as to the geographical origin of the good, and use which constitutes an act of unfair competition within the meaning of Article 10*bis* of the Paris Convention (Article 22.2).

The registration of a trademark which uses a geographical indication in a way that misleads the public as to the true place of origin must be refused or invalidated *ex-officio* if the legislation so permits or at the request of an interested party (Article 22.3).

Article 23 provides that interested parties must have the legal means to prevent the use of a geographical indication identifying wines for wines not originating in the place indicated by the geographical indication. This applies even where the public is not being misled, there is no unfair competition and the true origin of the good is indicated or the geographical indication is accompanied be expressions such as *kind, type, style, imitation* or the like. Similar protection must be given to geographical indications identifying spirits when used on spirits. Protection against registration of a trademark must be provided accordingly.

Geographical indication (GI) is one of the newest additions to the domain of IPRs. Being the youngest member of the IPR family, the research and dissemination among the stakeholders is still in a nascent stage. This book, it is hoped, would provide useful insights into issues related to intellectual property rights (IPRs), especially the domain of geographical indications (GIs).

Acknowledgements

We place on record our deep appreciation and gratitude to all the contributors to this volume for their scholarly research papers. We are grateful to Dr. P. Nayak, Secretary, Textiles Committee, Ministry of Textiles, Government of India, Mumbai, who guided us all the way and provided valuable suggestions at every stage of the completion of this book. Thanks are also due to Professor Ramakrushna Panigrahi of MATs Institute of Management, Bangalore and Dr. B.D. Majhi, Joint Director (Economics), Competition Commission of India, New Delhi for their co-operation and support.

Finally, we are thankful to the team of researchers of Market Research Wing, Textiles Committee for their continuous support and valued contributions.

Tapan Kumar Rout
Bidyadhar Majhi

1

Significance of GIs under TRIPS

Ramakrushna Panigrahi

Agreement on Trade Related Aspects of Intellectual Property Rights (TRIPS)

The Agreement establishing the World Trade Organization (WTO) contains, *inter alia*, an Agreement on Trade Related Aspects of Intellectual Property Rights (TRIPS).

TRIPS Agreement is Annex 1C of the Marrakesh Agreement establishing the World Trade Organization (WTO), signed in Marrakesh, Morocco on April 15, 1994.

The TRIPS Agreement, which came into effect on 1st January 1995, is to date, the most comprehensive multilateral agreement on intellectual property.

TRIPS provides for norms and standards in respect of the following areas of intellectual property:

1. Copyright and related rights (i.e. the rights of performers, producers of sound recordings and broadcasting organizations).
2. Trademarks including service marks.
3. Geographical indications including appellations of origin.
4. Industrial designs.
5. Patents including the protection of new varieties of plants.
6. Layout-designs of integrated circuits.
7. Undisclosed information including trade secrets and test data.
8. Control of anti-competitive practices in contractual licences.

Geographical Indications (GIs)

Geographical indications are defined, for the purposes of the Agreement, as indications which identify a good as originating in the territory of a Member, or a region or locality in that territory, where a given quality, reputation or other characteristic of the good is essentially attributable to its geographical origin (Article 22.1).

Thus, this definition specifies that the quality, reputation or other characteristics of a good can each be a sufficient basis for eligibility as a geographical indication, where they are essentially attributable to the geographical origin of the good.

In respect of all geographical indications, interested parties must have legal means to prevent use of indications which mislead the public as to the geographical origin of the good, and use which constitutes an act of unfair competition within the meaning of Article 10*bis* of the Paris Convention (Article 22.2).

The registration of a trademark which uses a geographical indication in a way that misleads the public as to the true place of origin must be refused or invalidated *ex-officio* if the legislation so permits or at the request of an interested party (Article 22.3).

Article 23 provides that interested parties must have the legal means to prevent the use of a geographical indication identifying wines for wines not originating in the place indicated by the geographical indication.

This applies even where the public is not being misled, there is no unfair competition and the true origin of the good is indicated or the geographical indication is accompanied by expressions such as “kind”, “type”, “style”, “imitation” or the like. Similar protection must be given to geographical indications identifying spirits when used in spirits. Protection against registration of a trademark must be provided accordingly.

Article 24 contains a number of exceptions to the protection of geographical indications. These exceptions are of particular relevance in respect of the additional protection for geographical indications for wines and spirits. For example, Members are not obliged to bring a geographical indication under protection, where it has become a generic term for describing the product in question (paragraph 6). Measures to implement these provisions shall not prejudice prior trademark rights that have been acquired in good faith (paragraph 5). Under certain circumstances, continued use of a geographical indication for wines or spirits may be allowed on a scale and nature as before (paragraph 4). Members availing themselves of the use of these exceptions must be willing to enter into negotiations about their continued application to individual geographical indications (paragraph 1). The exceptions cannot be used to diminish the protection of geographical indications that existed prior to the entry into force of the TRIPS Agreement (paragraph 3). The TRIPS Council shall keep under review the application of the provisions on the protection of geographical indications (paragraph 2).

GI may be defined as indications which identify goods as originating in the territory of a member country, or a region or locality in that territory, where a given quality, reputation or other characteristics of the said goods is essentially attributable to its geographical origin. In other words, some geographical regions acquire a reputation for origin of a product with some specific quality and uniqueness. It is this quality or reputation that distinguishes the goods from other similar products all over the world. When a geographical indication acquires such reputation, there may be attempts by others to use it to their own advantage.

Such actions by others harm both the producer as well as the consumers of the product. The original producer looses a part of the market while the consumer gets counterfeit goods which lack the quality and the originality of the product. Keeping these aspects in mind, GI has been included as an important IPR in TRIPS Agreement.

The Agreement has brought about a new dimension in the protection of intellectual property rights for the unique products (Article 22) and provides two levels of protection for the unique products originating from the specific geographical area with special characteristics. The general standard of protection stipulated in Article 22 is available to all products against deceptive or misleading business practices and other sorts of unfair competition, as and when the member country have a legal means to prevent it. On the other hand, Article 23 provides additional protection for the GI designated wines and spirits only. The additional protection stipulates that the member country should prevent any abusive application of such GIs, irrespective of whether the consumer mislead or it constitutes on act of unfair competition. The enhanced protection has turned out to be controversial as some countries consider the higher level of protection as discriminatory, while some other members endorse it. The controversy has arisen out of the interpretation of Article 24.1, which calls for multilateral negotiation on GI.

Geographical Indication of Goods (Protection and Registration) Act, 1999

In compilation to the TRIPS, agreement, the government of India has enacted the Geographical Indication of Goods (Protection and Registration) Act in 1999. The GI Act came into force on September 15, 2003 and provides ways and means for protecting the unique products through registration at national level. The Government of India also implemented the Geographical Indication Rules in 2002.

Since the signing up of TRIPS agreement, many member countries have enacted their own act for protecting the unique products originating from a geographical area through GI; many products have also been registered under the said acts. The EU is leading the table by protecting more than 2,500 products under the Protected Geographical Indication (PGI) and Protected of Designated Origin (PDO). India has also registered more than 170 products since the inception of the Act. With the registration of more and more products, the researchers have also tried to quantify the benefits of the registration by using different econometric tools and most of the studies have highlighted the positive impact of the registration of the unique products under the said act.

Potential Benefits of GIs

Internationally, researchers have tried to quantify the impact of the IPR protection of unique products and traditional knowledge (TK) through empirical research so as to quantify potential benefits of GI as an instrument for socio-economic development of the producers of the designated products. A consumer study organised by the EU Commission in 1999 has concluded that 40 percent of the consumers are willing to pay 10 percent premium per origin for the guaranteed products. The consumers' willingness to pay higher premium price to the original products may be attributed to the elimination of uncertainty on the quality and originality of product. A consumer study by EU Commission has further highlighted that GI provides value addition to the producers by facilitating product diversification and maintaining specific quality standards.

On product specific studies, the Jamaica Bru Mount coffee received a premium of US$ 14.50 per kg. in comparison to benchmark prices of Columbia miles. The French GI designated cheese has sold at a premium of 2 Euro per kg. over other non-protected cheese. Likewise, Italian Toscano Oil is also sold at a premium of 20 percent since it was registered as GI in 1998. Many of these products whose names are protected have experienced enhanced exports during the post-GI period. It has been estimated that 85 percent of French wine exports and 80 percent of EU exported spirits use GI as a marketing tool for promoting the product in export market. The GI has become a lifeline for 1,38,000 farms in France and 3,00,000 Italian employees for promoting their products and realising higher premium price, ultimately bringing socio-economic development of the products besides providing an important instrument for containment of infringement.

The studies on regional origins and prices of wine have also given rise to a positive impact of GI registration of the products. The primary econometric tool used in the analysis is the hedonic [1] pricing model on wine and it allows estimation of the value of such important features as a geographical origin, variety, vintage, etc. whose inclusion brings about an addition premium price for the original products. Schamel and Anderson (2003) extended this analysis to the case of Australian wines and found that regional origin has become a more important determinant of prices over a period (1992-2000).

Their study indicated that the average premium price of the product has increased by 31 percent in 2000s as compared to 1992 (the base price) for some Australian wines. Similarly, the Pinot Noir is cheaper by 22 percent compared to a Shiraz from the Barossa Valley, while a wine produced in Canberra is 25 percent more expensive than its counterparts because of GI. The significant differences in price during pre- and post-GI period may be attributed to the guarantee of the product's quality and originality through GI registration. Hence, the trends have pointed out that the products once registered can act as a riding force for better socio-economic development of the producers. Today, Italian producers are calling their "parama ham" as number one ham in Canada because of the protection under GI and its widespread appreciation and acceptance by the consumers in Canada.

GI as an IPR has given rise to multi-dimensional protection of the designated products. It protects the product from infringement by providing legal protection, which ultimately eliminates the unauthorised use of registered GI by unethical business practices. On the other hand, as evident from various impact studies, the protection helps in enhancing the value of the product by facilitating suitable market linkage and brand promotion. As such, it ultimately helps the stakeholders to enhance the marketability of the product. The increase in marketability brings about higher income for the producers and better quality product for consumers. It also standardises the quality and enhances the price. Hence, GI gives rise to legal protection of the product on one hand and brings about sustainable development of the producers on the other hand. This chapter has tried to explore the socio-economic implication of the IPR protection of unique products through GI along with the legal aspects associated with the registration of the product.

The main scope of the chapter is to bring an overview of GI Act and its effectiveness in protecting the unique products of the country. It has also highlighted the ways and means to protect the intangible assets of the stakeholders like weavers, master weavers, artisans, farmers etc. and means to convert the IPR protection into tangible benefits for emancipation of the socio-economic condition of the thousands of stakeholders associated with the products. The socio-cultural diversity of India has created many unique products and protection of these products can bring about new changes to their livelihood.

End Note

1. In hedonic models the observed market price of a product is the sum of the implicit (unobserved) prices paid for each attribute of the product. The assumption of these models is that the preferences (utility function) of consumers depend on the attributes of a product. Producers in term have cost functions, which depend on the attributes of the product. In equilibrium markets determine the implicit (unobserved) prices of these characteristics.

2

GIs in the Domain of Intellectual Property Rights (IPRs)

Tapan Kumar Rout

Background

Geographical indications (GIs) are one of the newest additions to the domain of intellectual property rights (IPRs) in the TRIPS Agreement. It identifies goods originality to a particular region with unique characteristics associated with the geo-climatic conditions, soil, water, cultural heritage or any other essential characteristics associated with it. With the expansion of global trade on traditional knowledge (TK) and creative economies in the recent years, the importance of these products has increased substantially. Prior to TRIPS agreements, countries, having realised the importance of these products, have been signed with an objective to preserve and protect the originality as conveyors of information to the consumers and facilitate its role as marketing tools. The TRIPS agreement under the framework of WTO is the latest and most comprehensive agreement in this regard to provide legal means to the member countries to prevent the misuse of intellectual property that deceive consumers and constitute as an act of unfair competition.

Historical Evolution of GI

In the pre-industrial age, when food and agriculture products were the principal output of the economies, certain regions of the world developed some specialties and reputation in the production of some goods. These goods are different to that of others in terms of quality, uniqueness, design or flavour. These specialised goods are presumed to be unique outcome of the geo-climatic conditions, soil, intellectual ability of the producer, or some specialty attached to that region derived from the socio-cultural ethos of the people of that place. In the process, these products are identified by the consumers in accordance with the name of region or origin. Some of such products are Darjeeling tea, Banaras Brocades and Saree, Kancheepuram silk of India, Parmaham, Feta Cheese of European Union, Iran Carpet, Pisco of Peru and China etc. These products are closely associated with the region of production in terms of deriving the name and also the unique quality associated with it. Hence, the producers of the designated products should have the right to use these indications as a means to achieve the premium price associated with it because of its origin and reputation.

It is believed that artisans of Egypt were the first users of region-derived indication when the brick makers used a mark to indicate the origin of the bricks and stones used for building pyramids. During that time, geographical indication was used as a sign of quality and strength of the stones. In ancient Greece, Thespian wine from the island of Thesos, in the Macedonia region, yielded a prime price of 20 drachmas for 20 litres for the unique quality. Even the use of GI for products like Parmigieno or Comté (also called Gruyère de Comté, a French cheese made from unpasteurized cow's milk in the Franche-Comté region of eastern France) dates back to the 13th century. As such, in the 13th century, the producers had tried to use the origin as a marketing tool for deriving the premium price associated with the products.

GI in the 20th Century

During the 20th century, countries protected their unique products, intertwining with commerce and industry, under the national laws enacted for the purpose. The national level initiatives taken up by the countries prior to the multilateral agreements [1] on GI can be defined under three major categories.

Protection Arising out of Legislative Provisions Established under the Jurisprudence: During the 20th century, France was the first country to enact a specific legislation for protecting the traditional knowledge (TK) through special industrial property rules called appellation of origin.

The French law enacted in 1919 recognized the existence of appellation of origin and laid down conditions for their protection. The appellation of origin was defined as consisting of name of the country, region and locality that serves to designate a product originating therein, the quality and characteristics of which are due to the geographical environment including natural and human factors. In other words, the products, which originated from a specific area having specific quality, can be protected under the law. In order to ensure the quality aspects, a control mechanism was also set up by the country, which stipulated quality control by inspection and issuing guidelines regularly. Only products, which comply with the quality standards stipulated under the national law were eligible for protection under the appellation origin. Initially, it was meant for products like wine, spirit, cheese, butter, poultry etc. but subsequently more products were also included in the list.

The popularity of the Law in France also induced other European countries to adopt similar kinds of law for protecting their products, particularly wine and spirits of their respective regions.

Certification Marks: The special title of protection promulgated by France was a public administrative initiative but did not talk about the private participation for protection. The collective mark [2] certification mark provided an important means for protection of GI, independent of statutory or judiciary measures. The concept of collective/certificate mark differed from country to country depending on the applicable law of the country. Once the designated products are registered as collective marks, the association/societies that own the marks have the right to prohibit its use by unauthorized persons. On the other hand, certification mark and guarantee marks are not owned by a collective body like the association but by a certification authority. [3] A certification mark may be used to certify, *inter alia* the origin of the products or services. The application for the registration of certification mark has to be accompanied by the regulations, which govern the use of certification mark.

Where a GI has been registered as a certification mark/guarantee mark, everybody whose products comply with the requirements set out in the regulation may normally use it. Such right to use however may not be in case of conflict with a senior right. The institution mark or the guarantee mark has the right to prohibit the use of that mark by producers, whose products do not comply with the requirements set out in the regulations. A special form of protected GI resembling the collective mark is the French "agriculture label".

Law of Unfair Competition: The original products acquire specific reputation due to its origin from a particular geographical region with specific qualities derived from geo-climatic condition or human skill associated with the process of production. The special characteristics associated with the products give rise to a premium price and often encourages dishonest business practices in the form of infringement. Such act misleads the consumers and is hence deceptive in nature. It also brings about misappropriation of the goodwill of the original manufacturers, who are truly entitled to use the GI.

Prior to TRIPS agreement, different countries have also enacted the law of unfair competition in order to stop such dishonest business practices. Under the provision of law, the use of GI on goods not originating from the respective area is misleading and the consumers are deceived as to the true place of origin and hence punishable.

Protection of GI through Provision of Bilateral Agreement

Initially, the countries tried to protect their respective GI through bilateral agreements. Many countries have entered into such agreements for protecting their designated GI in the respective countries during the 20th century. In general, such bilateral agreements provided protection to the designated products as per the pre-defined conditions and lists agreed upon by the countries. While negotiating on geographical indication, the countries have tried to put forth two important aspects for protection, i.e.:

1. To ensure the prohibition of the use of GI of other country in the national territory.
2. To allow the extra territorial application of other countries national law for protection of a geographical indication.

Some countries have also tried to ensure the protection of their geographical indications, while signing bilateral agreement with other countries. During 1960s, Germany and France agreed to protect the 'Indication of Source' and 'Appellation of Origin' in their respective countries so as to ensure effective protection of original products in their domestic markets. Similarly, Australia and the US also signed reciprocal agreements for protection of wine names in their domestic markets (1994). Even if the bilateral negotiation of GI had not proved as an effective solution to the products as a whole, it was a step in the right direction, in the absence of any multilateral agreement for protecting the original products.

GI in the Multilateral Agreement

The process of multilateral negotiation on GI started with the commencement of the Paris Convention in 1883 and since then, three important multilateral treaties have been signed during the 19th and early 20th century for protecting the GIs. The treaties are as follows:

1. The Paris Convention [4] for the protection of industrial property.
2. The Madrid Agreement [5] for the repression of false or deceptive indications of source on goods.
3. The Lisbon Agreement [6] for the protection of

appellations of origin and their international registration.

Paris Convention for the Protection of Industrial Property (1883): It was the first multilateral agreement on indication source. Since the adoption of Paris Convention in 1883, the convention have been revised four times and amended in 1979 for rendering the act more effective. The convention was initially signed by 11 countries and now has 171 contracting parties for protecting the indication of source (Article 1.2). Member countries of the Convention undertook to accept to file and protect collective marks belonging to foreign associations even in the absence of industrial/commercial establishment (Article 7*bis*). The Article 1(2) of the Convention included indications of source and applications of origin as subject matter of industrial property protection, while industrial property is defined, "all manufactured or natural products for example, wine, grain, tobacco test, fruits, cattle, minerals, mineral water and floor" [Article 1(3)].

Article 9 provides the remedies available in the event of import of goods unlawfully bearing a mark of trade name. Article 10(2) of the Convention stipulates that, "any producer, manufacturer or merchant whether a natural person or legal entity engaged in the production or manufacture of or trade in such goods and established either in the locality falsely indicated as the source or in the region where such locality is situated or in the country where the false indication or source is used, shall in any case be deemed as interested party".

The Convention, prohibits the "direct or indirect use of false indications of the sources of the goods" (Article 10.1) but no special provisions therein for the protection of appellations of origin; only *false indications* covered by Article 10 and no protection is provided for cases when the indication is used in a translated form or accompanied by terms such as "kind" or "type" or when it is deceptive, i.e. when it may mislead the public.

It is pertinent to mention that Articles 9(5) and 9(6) of the

Convention lay down conditions for agreed parties but whose national laws do not permit seizure or importation inside the country to replace those remedies by either prohibition or importation or by any other nationally available remedies. The condition was also again strengthened by Article 10(2) which stipulates an undertaking of the state parties to the Convention to allow federations and associations representing producers and trade circles to bring actions in order to enforce the means of protection as envisaged in Articles 9 and 10.

Madrid Agreement Concerning the International Registration of Marks (1891): The Madrid Agreement [7] was signed by 74 contracting parties and established a procedure for international registration of marks. Under the Agreement, protection was afforded to a mark based on national registration for 10 years, renewable indefinitely. In case the registration is cancelled for some reason or other in the country of origin within five years from international registration, the international mark can also be cancelled. The Agreement was also supplemented by the agreement on repression of false/deceptive indications of source of goods [8] in 1891. The Agreement aims at the repression of false and deceptive indications of source i.e. "all goods bearing a false or deceptive indication by which one of the countries to which this agreement applies, or a place situated therein, is directly or indirectly indicated as being the country or place of origin shall be seized on importation into any of the said countries" [Article 1(1)].

Article 1 defines the objective of the agreement as: (i) all goods bearings a false or deceptive indication to which the agreement applies or a place situated therein is directly or indirectly indicated as being the country or place of origin, shall be seized of importation into any of the said countries; (ii) seizure shall also affect in the country, where the false or deceptive indication of source has been applied for or into which the goods bearing the false or deceptive indication have been imported; (iii) if the laws of the country do not permit seizure upon importation, such seizure shall be replaced by prohibition of importation; (iv) if the laws of the country permit neither seizure upon importation, nor prohibition of importation to the country, then until such time as the laws are modified accordingly, those measures shall be replaced by the actions and remedies available in such case under the laws of such country; and (v) in the absence of any special sanctions ensuring the repression of false or deceptive indications of source, the sanctions provided by the corresponding provisions of the laws relating to marks or trade names shall be applicable.

Even with different other articles well defined within the scope and nature of protection, the Agreement failed to attract countries like the US, Germany and Italy.

As such, the Agreement failed in some extent to the non-endorsement of these countries.

Lisbon Agreement [9] for the Protection of Appellations of Origin and their International Registration 1958: The Lisbon Agreement was a result of Lisbon diplomatic conference in 1958, in which the member countries made an attempt to improve the international protection for geographical indications beyond the framework of Paris Convention and Madrid Agreement in terms of indication of source.

The Agreement stipulated for establishment of a special union for protection of appellation of origin registered at the International Bureau (Article 1). The Agreement stated:

1. Countries should undertake to protect the appellations of origin of products of the other countries of the special Union in their territories under the provision of Lisbon Agreement once registered at the International Bureau of Intellectual Property referred to in the Convention establishing the World Intellectual Property Organization (Article 1)—initially, 20 countries were the contracting parties for the convention.
2. Article 2 defines "appellations of origin" as the

geographical name of a country, region or locality, which serves to designate a product originating therein, the quality and characteristics of which are due exclusivcly or essentially to the geographical environment, including natural and human factors. Hence, the country of origin is the country whose name or the country in which is situated the region or locality whose name constitutes the appellation of origin which has given the product its reputation' (Article 2).

3. The Agreement has also ensured protection against any usurpation or imitation, even if the true origin of the product is indicated or if the appellation is used in translated form or accompanied by terms such as "kind", "type", "make", "imitation" or the like (Article 3).
4. Once protected in a country, an appellation of origin cannot be deemed to have become generic in that country, as long as it is protected as an appellation of origin in the country of origin (Article 6).

The main theme of the Lisbon Agreement on appellation of origin is to protect the producers that possess special characteristics and factors of quality attributable to its geographical origin. For the purpose, geographical indication means, 'the name of the country, region or locality which serves to designate a product originated theme and the quality and characteristics of which are due exclusively or essentially to the geographical environment, including natural and human factors' [Article 2(1)]. The essential requirements to protect a product are:

1. It should be protected in the country of origin.
2. It should be registered in the international register of VIPs.

However, the Agreement did not make exception for geographical indications which are already generic.

Provisions of TRIPS Agreement on GI

The Agreement on the Trade Related Intellectual Property Rights (TRIPS) under WTO is the first multilateral agreement to provide an explicit definition of the term "geographical indication. [10]". The Agreement defines GI (Article 22.1) as, "indications which identify goods as originating in the territory of a member country or a region or locality in that territory, where a given quality, reputation or other characteristic of the good is essentially attributed to its geographical origin". Hence, the term GI accommodates both appellation of origin and indications of source of Lisbon and Madrid agreements while defining GI. As such, GI can be defined as a distinct sign/indication, which identifies a good;

1. Originating in a specified territory or region or locality in that territory.
2. Where a specific quality, reputation or other characteristics of the goods is given.
3. It is essentially associated to geographical area of origin.

The provision establishes a minimum standard of protection (Article 22) for all mandating members to provide the legal means of protection for interested parties to prevent the use of GIs in a manner which misleads the public as to the true origin of the good as well as acts of unfair competition.

The general norm of protection (Article 22.2) stipulates that, "all the members shall provide legal means for interested parties to prevent the use of any means in the designation and/or presentation of goods that indicates that the good in question originates in a geographical area other than the true place of the origin or any use which constitutes an act of unfair competition within the meaning of Article 10*bis* of the Paris Convention (1967)." The provisions of Article 22.3 [11] and Article 22.4 [12] supplements Article 22.2, which states that in respect of GIs, for goods not originating in the territory indicated, if the use of those trademarks for such goods would be misleading as to the true place of origin of the goods, the remedy that must be available in that situation is refusal or invalidation of the trademark registration, either ex-officio, if the applicable law so allows, or at the request of an interested party.

Article 23.1 provides for additional protection to wines and spirits only. It reads as, "each member shall provide the legal means for interested parties to prevent the use of a GI identifying wines not originating in place indicated in question or identifying spirits not originating in place indicated by the GI in question, even where the true origin of the goods is indicated or the geographical indication is used in translation or accompanied by the expression such as 'kind', 'type', 'imitation' or the like". Further, the Article has stipulated that "notwithstanding the first sentence of Article 24, members may, with respect to these obligations, instead provide for enforcement by administrative action". Further, Article 23.1 is supplemented by a paragraph dealing specifically with the registration of trademarks for wines containing or consisting of a geographical indication for spirits, where the wines and spirits in question do not have the indicated geographical origin. Registration of trademarks falling under that provision has to be refused or cancelled, either ex-officio if the applicable law so allows, or at the request of an interested party. Besides, the Agreement also provides a series of exceptions, most notably in relation to continued and similar use of GIs for wines and spirits, prior good faith trademark rights and generic designations (Article 24).

Insufficiency of General Protection

In contrast to Article 22, Article 23 of the Agreement stipulates an additional protection for GIs designating wines and spirits only, which requires member countries to prevent any abusive application of such GIs irrespective of whether the consumers are misled or it constitutes an act of unfair competition. Using a GI identifying wines/spirits for wines/spirits not originating in the place indicated by the concerned is prohibited, even where the true origin of the wine/spirit concerned is indicated and/or a translation is used and/or the indication is accompanied by expressions such as 'kind', 'type', 'style', 'imitation' or the like (Article 23.1). As such, the provision disallows the producers not producing in the geographical region purported in GI associated with wines or spirits to use such an indication in their trademarks (Article 23.2). In contrast, the refusal or invalidation of registration of a trademark for any other goods (than wines and spirits), on similar ground, is conditional on the 'misleading test' (Article 22.3). [13]

Unlike the 'absolute' and unconditional protection of goods (Article 23) for designating wines and spirits, Article 22 stipulates general level of protection to other designated products. The misleading test prescribed for the wine and spirits do not apply for other products. In such circumstances, the Agreement has given the responsibility to prove the misleading test on producers of the original product. It means, the original producers have to prove that the misuse of the designated GI by any other producers not representing the original one, mislead the public as the geographical origin of the product or must constitute an act of unfair competition. This requirement of the so-called 'misleading test', which can, at best be regarded as suitable in preventing unfair competition or consumer protection regulations, fails to provide a sufficient intellectual property protection for the legitimate users of GI. It does not prevent a producer from using a GI for his product, even if it does not originate in the territory purported, as long as the product's true origin is indicated on the label.

For instance, a brocade producer from Bangladesh and Pakistan may use the world famous appellation 'Banaras' on the package of his *saree* with the aim of free-riding on the goodwill and reputation associated with it and still claim that he is not 'misleading' the public simply by mentioning true origin of his product somewhere in the package, even if it is done in a manner which is likely to go unnoticed by the buyers. Thus, Article 22 allows misappropriation of renowned GIs without violating the law. Furthermore, in stark contrast with Article 23, Article 22 does not prevent the use of GIs in translation or with accompaniment of expressions such as 'style', 'type', 'kind', 'imitation' or the like.

For instance, even if someone in Punjab makes a sparkling wine with taste and texture identical with those of 'Champagne' wine of France, the provision of Article 23 does not permit him to sell his product as 'Champagne from Punjab' or 'Champagne-type wine from Punjab' etc. The absence of such an effective shield to the products other than wine and spirit creates a wide gap in providing effective protection to the products other than wine and sprit. This may be the factor why, India could not prevent, a Texas-based company from selling rice produced in America as 'traditional basmati style' or 'American basmati', in contrast to the original basmati which originates from the Indian sub-continent.

The allowance of such use, however, puts the GI concerned, at the risk of becoming a 'generic name [14]' over a period of time. Geographical names such as 'French' fries or 'Bermuda' or even, 'Rasgola' became generic even if these products have originated from a particular geographical region as their respective right holders did not take initiatives to protect them. By regulating production and delimiting the area of production, they have lost their claim as the original producer of these products over a period of time and have become common names for particular categories of goods which, no longer originated from France or Bermuda or Bengal only.

The net result of this discriminatory approach is that, excepting the GIs denominating wines and spirits, all other GIs run the risk of being wrongfully exploited by the dishonest business practices for taking away premium price associated with the reputation or goodwill of the original product and making these products generic over a period of time.

The requirement of the 'misleading test' also leads to legal uncertainty on protection and enforcement of individual GI at the international level. The test stipulates that, "it is up to the national courts and national administrative authorities to decide whether the public is being misled by a particular abuse of a GI and to enforce their decisions". Since, such judgments are bound to differ from country to country, the very provision of the 'misleading test' leaves room for legal uncertainty and inconsistent decisions. This is not the case with GIs designating wines and spirits.

Further, as per the misleading test, it is up to the plaintiff to prove before the judicial or administrative authorities that the public has been misled. No such burden of proof has been put on the producer (the plaintiff) in the domain of GIs designating wines or spirits and the net result of this discriminatory approach is that except the GI denominating wines and spirits, all other goods run the risk of being wrongfully exploited in the international arena. Hence, it is evident that the TRIPS agreement has taken special care for wines and spirits, while putting other products in a protection basket, which is not at par with these two products.

Exceptions to GI under TRIPS

Article 24 stipulates certain exceptions to GI. It may be attributed to the agreement among the members to provide a platform to the countries to engage in negotiations for enhanced protection of GIs under Article 23. The exceptions and concessions recognise the so-called 'acquired rights' prior to agreement. The exception [15] is talking about prior and continued use of GIs that have become generic. The exceptions are as follows:

1. If a name has been used for at least 10 years preceding the conclusion of the Uruguay Round or in "good faith" for a shorter period of time preceding that date, the user can continue to do so (Article 24.4).
2. Trademark will remain valid if it has been registered in good faith prior to the TRIPS Agreement, or if it has been registered before the GI was protected in its country of origin (Article 24.5 and Article 24.7).
3. When a GI becomes a common term for the type of goods in the language of a particular member state (i.e. generic),

protection must no longer be accorded in that State (Article 24.6).

4. The protection of GIs does not prevent a person whose name corresponds to a geographical indication to use that name in their commercial operations as long as that name is not being used in any misleading way (Article 24.8).
5. There is no obligation to protect geographical indications which are not, or have ceased to be, protected in their country of origin or which have fallen into disuse in that country.

The first exception (Article 24.4) gives the right to WTO members to allow continued and similar use of a particular geographical indication of another member identifying wine or sprits, in connection with goods or services by any of its nationals or domiciliary who have used that geographical indication in a continuous manner with regard to the same or related goods or services in the territory of the Member, either for at least 10 years preceding April 15, 1994, or in good faith preceding that date.

The second exception relates to rights in trademarks (Article 24.5). It basically states that the implementation of the section on geographical indications by WTO members is without prejudice to the registration of trademarks identical with or similar to geographical indication, to the application for registration of such trademarks, or the right to use such trademarks, if the following conditions are fulfilled: (a) an application for the registration of such trademarks must have been filed, or the trademark must have been registered, or (b) where the right to the trademark was acquired by use, that trademark must have been used, in good faith, in the WTO members before the agreement became applicable in that Member, or before the geographical indication in question is protected in its country of origin.

The third exception (Article 24.6) is related to geographical indications of a WTO member, which are considered by another member to be a term customary in common language as the common name for goods or services or, where the geographical indication is used for products of the wine, it is identical with the customary name of a grape variety existing in the territory of that member as of the date of entry into force of the Agreement.

One of the important components of agreement is that the protection must be sought on a country-by-country basis and hence does not come automatically. Further, a member country cannot ask for protection in other countries unless and until the product get protected in the country of origin. However, these exceptions are open to bilateral or multilateral negotiations if and when the member countries so desire and leaving countries to conclude agreements bilaterally as per the requirement of national territories.

Multilateral Negotiations: A Matter of Debate under Doha Development Round

Convinced of the vulnerability of the GIs designated products other than spirits and wines, India along with a host of other like-minded [16] countries has been continuously raising the issue in the WTO forum for quite some time, for an extension of the ambit of absolute protection to other unique products.

These countries question the basis of such a differential treatment to products other than wines and spirits and points out the inadequacy of Article 22 serving the purpose, which allows competitors, not belonging to the geographical region purported by a GI, to easily 'usurp' a GI and free-ride on its reputation without leaving any scope for the legitimate right holders to prevent such misappropriation as long as the true origin of the product is mentioned. According to their argument, producer of any good and not only those of wines or spirits have a legitimate right in protecting their respective GIs from such exploitation. Hence, all GIs, irrespective of the product category, should be accorded protection both under Article 22 and Article 23 of the TRIPS agreement without differentiating the products on the basis of level of protection.

On the other hand, countries like the United States, Australia, New Zealand, Canada, Argentina, Chile, Guatemala, and Uruguay etc. are against such an 'extension' of additional protection as given to wines and spirits, to other products. This group against the extension of protection is of the opinion that the existing level of protection under Article 22 is adequate and providing enhanced protection to other products would be an expensive proposition. Furthermore, they perceive that a better protection to other products could act as a barrier to trade as it may give rise to relabeling the designated products. They also reject the 'usurping' accusation put forward by the proponents of the extension on the pretext that migrants have taken the methods of making the products and the names with them to their new homes. For this reason, the debate has very often been described as the one between the 'Old versus New World'. It is pertinent to note that the debate on 'extension' cuts across the traditional 'North-South' divide as it exists in most of the IPR-related issues.

GI Negotiation on Doha Development Round

The issue of 'extension' was a part of the discussions in the fourth Ministerial Conference of the WTO at Doha (held in November 2001), which marked the beginning of a new round of trade talks called the 'Doha Development Round'. In particular, paragraph 18 of the Doha Declaration notes that the "*...issues related to the extension of the protection of geographical indications provided for in Article 23 to products other than wines and spirits will be addressed in the Council for TRIPS pursuant of paragraph 12 of this declaration*". As such, the WTO member countries are continuing negotiation on various issues pertaining to GI.

Notably, Paragraph 12 of the Doha Declaration declared that the negotiations on outstanding 'implementation issues' shall be an integral part of the Doha work programme. It further states that: (a) those issues, on which the Doha

Declaration provides a specific negotiating mandate, shall be addressed under that mandate, whereas, (b) the other outstanding implementation issues shall be addressed as a matter of priority by the relevant WTO bodies, which shall report to the Trade Negotiations Committee (TNC) for appropriate action.

The member countries participating in the ongoing debate in the TRIPS Council on the issue of 'extension' have failed to reach any consensus even on the question of whether Paragraph 12 of the Doha Declaration provides a mandate for negotiations on this matter. Many countries [17] are of the opinion that the so-called outstanding implementation issues are already part of the negotiation, while others maintain that these issues could only be a part of negotiation if and when the Trade Negotiating Committee (TNC) decides. As of now, the stalemate in the council is continuing.

The complications have been further accumulated by the attempt of countries like the EU, Switzerland and Bulgaria to link movement on 'extension' to negotiations on agriculture. Their feeling is that any progress in this issue would make it easier for them to agree for a significant deal in agriculture. It is an anomaly that different levels of protection is granted by the agreement according to product categories in GIs only in spite of the fact that it stands on an equal footing with any other IPR. Also, there are no logical or legal reasons, which could justify the discriminatory treatment between GIs associated with wines or spirits to those of other products.

The discriminatory approach towards GIs can only be explained in the light of the negotiating history of the TRIPS Agreement. The provision is the result of trade-offs among the countries at the time of Uruguay Round negotiations, particularly during the Brussels Ministerial Conference (1990). It appears that the higher level of protection was granted solely for persuading the European Union (EU) to join for consensus on the Uruguay Round package, in spite of strong opposition from many countries.

On the other hand, Article 24 is the direct outcome of difficult negotiations between a number of wine-producing participants, notably in the EU, that wished to protect the indications for wines and spirits fully, on the one hand and others that were afraid that it might affect rights more or less considered to be 'acquired rights' in certain appellations, on the other. The result of the negotiations was only partly satisfactory for both sides, because, though protection was granted, it was done not exactly in the way proposed by the former group. Similarly, on safeguards for 'acquired rights' as included in the agreement, it was neither complete nor permanent in nature.

The only feasible option not blocking the negotiation was thus to agree to further talks. Hence, Article 24.1 provided that, *"Members agree to enter into negotiations aimed at increasing the protection of individual geographical indications under Article 23"*. Moreover, since safeguards for 'acquired rights' were included in Article 24, negotiators clearly indicated in Article 24.1 that:

1. Those safeguards should not be used to impede negotiations, and
2. In the context of such negotiations, the continued applicability of the safeguards should be possible for individual indications.

This is consistent with the establishment of a registration system, as has been proposed for wines and spirits under Article 23.4, where each individual indication entered in the registry might have to be negotiated. The negotiation on the establishment of a multilateral system of notification and registration of GIs for wines and spirits has been going on in the TRIPS Council since July 1997 and is yet to see any concrete progress.

Even if extensive discussions have taken place on extending the scope of additional protection correctly available for wines and spirits, serious difference of opinion exists among the members. Further, wary about the re-opening of negotiations under the Doha round, the members have decided to concentrate on four issues, i.e. agriculture, Non-Agricultural Market Access (NAMA), Singapore issues and cotton and hence, GI as an issue of negotiation has been pushed back.

GI and Legal Framework in India

Prior to GI Act, 1999: Prior to the enactment of the Geographical Indication (Protection and Registration) of Goods Act, 1999 by the Indian Parliament, the designated products in India enjoyed some sort of protection under different national laws like: (i) Consumer Protection Act, (ii) through passing off [18] actions in courts, and (iii) through certification marks.

Under the common law of 'passing off', any aggrieved person can file an action of 'passing off' to prevent another person from misrepresenting the aggrieved person's goods or services as that of his own. The court depends heavily on established case laws governing passing off in India. In case of original products, an action of passing off could be resorted to by the aggrieved person for the protection of his right, on the grounds that the brand value or the originality of his product is misutilised by some other producers for their own advantage and hence misleading the consumers.

The courts in India have applied same principle while pronouncing different verdicts during the past. In *Ellora Industries vs Banarsi Dass*, the Delhi High Court pronounced an important judgement on the concept and scope of 'passing off' action. In paragraph 35 of the judgment, the court observed that the purchasers were likely to be misled by the conception that the defendant's firm had an intimate connection with the plaintiffs and even misrepresentation of some connection with the plaintiffs was sufficient to constitute an act of unfair trading, now forming part of the law of passing off. As such, the case revealed that Indian courts have maintained the action of passing off to protect original products during the time when no specific act was available to protect the designated geographical indication.

Similarly, in the case of *Scotch Whisky Association vs. Pravara Sahakar Karkhana Ltd.* AIR 1992 Bom 294, the plaintiff [19] instituted the passing off action against the defendants [20], who manufacture and sell blended scotch, whisky in the name of 'Drum Beater' and 'Gold Tycoon'.

After examining the facts, the Bombay High Court held that:

1. The plaintiff has sufficient interest and *locus standi* to prevent passing off of Indian whisky manufactured by defendant as 'Scotch whisky' and to prevent the damage to goodwill and reputation associated with original Scotch whisky.
2. The plaintiffs have made out a strong prima facie case that the defendant is passing off their product as Blended Scotch whisky that is closely associated with the original whisky, which is not true. The plaintiffs have, therefore, made out a case for grant of an interim injunction on merits of the case.
3. The defendant is intentionally passing off their product as "Blended Scotch" although as a matter of law, even unintentional misrepresentation is actionable.
4. The defendant is restrained from advertising or offering for sale the whisky, which is not Scotch whisky with the description "Blended with Scotch whisky" or "Blended Scotch whisky" or "Blended with six year old scotch" or "Blended with six year old Vatted malt Scotch" or the word "scotch" or the impugned labels or impugned carton which bear the mark "Gold Tycoon" containing the word "Scotch" or the description Blended Scotch Whisky" or "Blended with six years".

From the aforesaid judgment, it is evident that the judiciary in India has provided adequate protection to the unique products originating from a particular geographical area in the absence of any specific legislation on GI. Hence, it is significant to note that such protection was accorded to the products in India much before the TRIPS Agreement came into force under the framework of WTO.

In another such case, the national judiciary tried to address an important pertinent question on GI i.e., 'Can geographical name, without any relevance to the trade be registered as a trademark?'. This issue was addressed in *Imperia Tobacco Co. of India vs. Registrar of Trademarks of India [21]*. In this case, the Imperia Tobacco Company of India filed an application before the Registrar of Trademarks for IPR protection of a logo under the Trade Mark Act. The trademark filed for registration was a label used as a wrapper for the packet of cigarettes which bore the device of snow-covered hills outlined with the word "Simla". The label was prominently written in various panels of the label with a small inscription that the content is a product of the appellant company. The Registrar rejected the application for registration due to the geographical affiliation of the word Shimla. Upon rejection of the application, the company filed an appeal before the Calcutta High Court for providing relief in this regard. The Calcutta High Court while disallowing the appeal made by the tobacco company observed the following:

1. The mark "Simla" is a geographical name and the outline of snow-clad hills in the mark indicates its use in ordinary or geographical signification, so that the mark is neither a fancy or invented word nor one with a secondary meaning.
2. A word is not debarred from registration merely because it is geographical name. Some geographical names can be inherently adapted to distinguish the goods of particular traders, but only if it can be predicated that they are such names as it would never occur to any other trader in such goods to use.
3. No trademark should be allowed to be registered which may hamper or embarrass the traders or trade, now or in future in respect of the place or country which is proposed to be registered.
4. In view of the imprint of snow-clad hills in the trademark

"Simla", the ordinary or geographical signification is obvious even though it has no reference to the quality or place of origin of goods. Further, registration of such trademark may hamper or embarrass the trade or traders in or around the locality in future as held by judicial authorities cited earlier in similar cases. Also "Simla" is too prominent a city, the capital of Himachal Pradesh, well known in the country and abroad and in its ordinary geographical significance is inherently neither distinctive nor adapted to distinguishing the goods of the appellant as a particular trader from those of others, and is also hit by the provisions of Section 9 sub-section (1), CI (d) of Section 9 of the Trade and Merchandise Marks Act, 1958.

Existing Remedial Measures against Infringement

One of the important provisions for IPR protection of original products through GI is the containment of infringement.

The infringements allow the dishonest business practices to free ride on the goodwill and reputation of the original products and deceive consumers by producing and marketing the counterfeit grade in the name of original one.

Prior to the GI Act, different Indian national laws have provided some sort of protection against infringement. Under the Indian judiciary system, the court may grant civil remedies like: (i) injunction, (ii) damages, and (iii) account of profit. The order of injunction may include: (i) an ex-parte injunction; or (ii) any interlocutory order for any of the following matters, namely: (a) for discovery of documents; (b) preserving or infringing goods, documents or other evidence which are related to the subject matter of the suit; and (c) restraining the defendant from disposing or dealing with his assets in manner, which may adversely affect plaintiff's ability to recover damages, costs or other pecuniary remedies which may be finally awarded to the plaintiff.

Interlocutory Injunction: It is a well settled law that in granting or not granting an interim injunction, three factors have to be kept in view, namely: (i) the establishment of prima facie case, (ii) the balance of convenience between the parties, and (iii) if the interim injunction is not issued, it will cause, irrespirable injury to the applicant. In India, courts have held in a series of cases that an interlocutory injunction will not generally be granted: (i) where damage will provide an adequate remedy; and (ii) unless there is a real probability of the plaintiff succeeding on the trial of the suit.

Final Injunction: The plaintiff will normally be entitled to a permanent injunction to restrain future infringements, if he succeeds at the trial in establishing infringement of GIs.

Damages: Under the provisions, the aggrieved party may seck damagc from thc infringcr for infringcmcnt of her intellectual property. The court may grant nominal damage to the aggrieved parties. However, the court shall not grant relief by way of damages (other than nominal damages) on account of profits in any case:

Where in a suit for infringement, the defendant satisfies that: (i) at the time he commenced to use the GIs complained of in the suit, he was unaware and had no reasonable ground for believing that GIs of the plaintiff was on the register and that when he became aware of the existence and nature of the plaintiff's right in the GIs, hence forthwith ceased to use the GIs in relation to goods in respect of which it was registered;

Where in a suit for passing off, the defendant satisfies: (i) that at the time he commenced the use of the GIs complained of in the suit, he was unaware and had no reasonable ground for believing that GIs relating to the plaintiff was in use and that when he became aware of the existence and the nature of the GIs relating to the plaintiff he forthwith ceased to use the GIs complained of.

However, such legal provisions were far from adequate to provide effective protection for the precious unique products originating from a particular geographical region of our country. This becomes evident from the manner in which innumerable dishonest business practices have been found to be free riding on the goodwill and reputation associated with such renewed geographical names, for years. For example, the famous 'Pochampally Ikat' of Andhra Pradesh was being copied by some textile mills and power looms and they marketed the counterfeit product in the name of 'Pochampally Ikat' for taking away the premium price associated with original one. Similarly, the famous 'Chanderi Saree' of Madhya Pradesh was produced and marketed in South India as South Chanderi Saree in order to sell it to the consumers in the protest of original Chanderi.

In order to address such issues of infringement and provide a more realistic safeguard to the unique products, the inclusion of GI as an important component of TRIPS Agreement was a step in the right direction.

Geographical Indication (GI) Act, 1999

In compliance with the TRIPS Agreement, the Indian Parliament enacted the *Geographical Indications of Goods (Registration and Protection) Act in 1999 and Rules in 2000.* The act stipulated provisions to register and protect original and unique products of the country for protecting the interests of both the producer group and the consumers. The main objective was to safeguard the interest of producers as well as the consumers from being deceived by falsity of geographical origin.

It is expected that the act would also facilitate the socio-economic development of the producer and help in promoting the GIs in both domestic and international market. Further, the provision in TRIPS agreement that a member country is not obliged to provide protection to other GI countries unless and until the product is protected in the country of origin (Article 22) may have also prompted the government to enact the act in the country. Hence, a specific GI act is not only a pre-requisite for protecting the designated products in the domestic market but is also helpful in seeking protection in other member countries. Countries like India has an important stake in the protection, as it is a richly endowed with natural and agricultural products like 'Darjeeling' (tea), 'Alphonso' (mango), 'Basmati' (rice), Banaras (Brocades and Saree) and a host of other products. The enactment of the GI Act has established a much needed mechanism for protection of these unique products of the country.

To govern the Act, the Indian government established the 'Geographical Indications Registry' with an all-India jurisdiction at Chennai, where the rightholders could register their respective products. The Act is administered by the Controller General of Patents, Designs and Trade Marks, who is the Registrar of Geographical Indications. Once the product is registered, a person or an association of producers claiming to be the producer of the designated good can file an application for registration as registered proprietor and can acquire the legal ownership of the product in form of registration of the product.

Provisions of TRIPS Agreement, GI Act of India

It is interesting to note that though Article 23 of TRIPS accords a higher level of protection to GIs denominating wines and spirits only, the corresponding provisions in the Indian act does not restrict themselves to wines and spirits only. It has been left to the discretion of the government to decide which goods or classes of goods should be granted such a high level of protection. This discrepancy has deliberately been maintained by the lawmakers of India with an aim to ensure 'absolute' protection (Article 23) for the GIs, having export potential for the country at least in the domestic market. It should be noted here that since the TRIPS agreement merely stipulates the 'minimum' standards of protection that the member countries of the WTO are obliged to accord for any IPR, India is free to extend the ambit of the 'absolute' protection to cover products other than wines and spirits, to the extent that it is not in contravention of the provisions of TRIPS

Agreement.

With the enactment of the act, legitimate users of geographical denomination, could go all out to ensure the 'absolute' level of protection for their respective GIs. This is a necessary condition that needs to be fulfilled on the domestic front to protect the prized GIs of the country from any future IPR-theft in the international arena, because, according to Article 24.9 of TRIPS, member countries do not have any obligation whatsoever to protect the GIs, which are not so protected in their respective countries of origin.

The sufficient condition, however, is definitely an extension of the 'absolute' level of protection, currently afforded by TRIPS only to GIs designating wines and spirits, to cover all other GIs because, in its current status, the TRIPS does not impose any obligation on the member countries of the WTO to ensure the 'absolute' protection for the GIs of Indian origin in their respective countries. However, without such 'absolute' protection, these appellations cannot be safeguarded completely in the international front.

Procedure for IPR Protection in India

The GI Act, 1999 and GI Rules, 2002 adopted a specific procedure for registering unique products in the country. The responsibility of administering the act has been assigned to the Controller General of Patents, Designs and Trademarks, who is appointed by the Government as Registrar [22] of the GI Act.

The Act stipulates registration in two parts, i.e.:

1. Part A for registration of designated products and the associations/consortium of the product as registered proprietors, and
2. Part B for registration of producers as authorised users.

The act protects manufactured/agricultural/natural goods, which originated from specific geographical area having specific unique quality derived from geo-climatic conditions or from the human skills of the producers associated with the production of the product. Unlike other instruments of IPRs like patents, and trademarks, geographical indications envisages community ownership, whereby the entire community associated with the production, distribution, marketing or working for the development of the product could acquire the legitimate ownership right by registering the products through GI Act. Since the Act stipulates the involvement of entire community, the procedure involved in the process of registration is complex and time consuming than other instruments of IPR.

The application for registration of a product shall be made in the prescribed form, [23] accompanied by requisite fee. The applicant can file the application in triplicate along with statement of case accompanied by five additional representations before the Registrar of GI for registration. The procedures for registering the product could be summarised as follows.

Procedure for Filing Application

Identification of Stakeholders: GI as an IPR is in a very early stage of implementation in India. The producers associated in the process of production are not aware of the pros and cons of the GI Act. In most of the cases, the stakeholders are not aware of their rights being treated out of their intellectual abilities of their forefathers and the importance of registration of such products through legal means. Hence, it is necessary to identify the real stakeholders for initiating process of registration. Further, most of the products bear generational legacy and are closely associated with the socio-cultural ethos of the society.

The stakeholders could be producers, support service providers like distributors, suppliers of raw materials, traders, exporters and government agencies etc. working for the development of the product. For the sake of the convenience, they may be segregated into following three categories:

1. **Grassroot Level Stakeholders:** The manufacturers associated with the production and distribution of the

product at the central level can be categorised as grassroot level stakeholders, e.g. in case of unique textiles, the weavers, master weavers, designers based at the production centre, dyers, processors, traders, exporters, who are providing support service in the process of production can be categorised in this segment.

2. **Blue Collar:** The civil society organisations and different associations including developmental agencies are continuously working for the development of the grassroots level stakeholders and the products as well. Their presence in the production centre is also equally important for the betterment of the producers. Hence, their role is of utmost importance for the economic well-being and empowerment of the grassroot level stakeholders and for bringing visibility of the product in the world market.
3. **White Collar:** The government agencies [24], and other developmental associations are also working round the corner for the development of the product. Their contribution for increasing the production base and marketability of the product in the present globalised market structure is also equally important for the sustainability of the product and hence can be considered as white collar stakeholders.

In the process of registration, all these above mentioned stakeholders play a crucial role in registration and effective protection of the product. Hence, their participation in the process of registration under the said Act is utmost necessary.

Capacity Building of the Stakeholders

Even if the Act does not stipulate the creation of awareness as one of the pre-requisites for filing an application, it is one of the important facets for IPR protection of a designated product. GI stipulates community ownership—as the designated products are mostly produced by a community. In this context, it is necessary to make them aware of the different aspects of the Act and how the registration is going to benefit them. In India, the stakeholders of most of the designated products like traditional knowledge, unique textiles, handicrafts etc. are economically backward and not well acquainted with the rules of registration.

In such a scenario, without their active participation in the process, it may be difficult to bring about an effective protection through registration. Therefore, the capacity building of the stakeholders seems to be an indispensable pre-requisite for developing a mechanism to protect the designated products. However, efforts should be made to bring all the stakeholders to a single fold so that their concerns can be recorded and a platform could be created for filing an application.

The awareness initiatives should address the issues like identifying potential applicants for filing application, creating a platform consisting of all stakeholders for taking up the initiatives, formation of the consortium with the inclusion of all products and sensitizing the state governments and other developmental agencies working for the development of the producers.

Formation of Consortium

Consortium is an association of two or more individuals or companies and/or organisations, associations, co-operative societies created with an objective to achieve common and mutually agreeable goals. Basically, the consortium should be a legal entity/open industry forum formed for mutual execution of some pre-determined activities.

Since these historically originated products are produced by a community of stakeholders, there is a need to bring the entire stakeholders under one-fold by constituting a consortium consisting of all stakeholders and their association. The formation of consortium is not mandatory under the Act but seems to be necessary for serving the interest of the stakeholders in a better way and undertaking post-GI initiatives including the containment and infringement for social and economic emancipation of the producer community.

For the purpose, all stakeholders involved either in the process of production, marketing or for the development of the products can be a member of consortium. Members of the consortium could be:

1. Manufacturers of the products and/or their associations.
2. Traders/exporters involved in the process of marketing the product and/or their associations.
3. Non-governmental organisations (NGOs) working for the development of the stakeholders' products.
4. Government organisations (Central or State) actively participating for the development and growth of the product.

The main objective of the consortium may be: (a) to protect the product through GI Act and devise strategy for optimising the benefits of IPR protection through brand promotion and market linkage so that the protection could be transferred into tangible benefits for the producers in terms of increase in income, creation of more employment and enhanced productivity.

The consortium should be a legal entity as the ownership of the product would be vested with it. In case of infringement, the consortium is supposed to take the legal action against the infringer. Therefore, the consortium should be registered under a suitable existing Indian Act. [25]

Study and Documentation

The very definition of the Act indicates that the goods which originate/manufactured in a particular territory of the country/ region/locality in that territory having given quality, reputation or other characteristics associated with the geographical area, are eligible for registration. It means that products should have some unique characteristics with respect to quality or reputation associated with that particular area for seeking registration. For example, in case of Darjeeling Tea, the flavour is associated with the altitude and the quality of soil of that particular area of the country and is not found in any other tea in the world. Hence, the quality and the flavour of the tea are closely associated with the geo-climatic condition of that area. Further, the Act stipulates that the product should have originated from that particular area of the country. Besides, the production process, the stakeholders, the area of marketing of the products, the inspection mechanism, specifications along with the production process and the raw materials used in the process of production should be clearly defined for registering a product under the said Act. Therefore, it is imperative that an exhaustive study and documentation should be undertaken before filing the application. The study should mainly focus on the following issues:

1. Identifying the historical origin of the product with written proofs. In case of non-availability of the written proofs of origin, the applicant should record the origin of the product from the stakeholders or from any unpublished available source.
2. The different stages of production along with photographs should be collected. Every effort should be made to record the specifications of raw materials used in the process of production along with the products.
3. The uniqueness of the products should be established with a proof that it has been accumulated from the geo-climatic condition of the product or due to the human skills associated in the process of production or any other parameters.
4. The geographical spread of the production centre should also be identified along with the authenticated maps, so that no producer is left out.
5. Every effort should be made to rope in each and every stakeholder involved in the process of production or distribution of the product. No stakeholders should be left out in the process of documentation, as it may create legal uncertainty for him while implementing the protection issues.

6. The inspection mechanism for maintaining the quality of the product in the post-registration period should also be identified.
7. Socio-economic conditions of the stakeholders needs to be elaborated and efforts should be made to define why GI registration is essential for the product and how it will be helpful for the stakeholders.

Besides helping the registration process, the study and documentation could act as a database for the product for containment of infringement.

Preparation of Application

Based on the documentation of the product, an application should be prepared in the prescribed format which should include the historical origin, geographical area of production, production process with specification and uniqueness along with the inspection mechanism for protecting the quality of the producer in post-GI registration period.

Application for Registration	
Part A of the GI register	Section (191), Rule 23(2)
Part A of the GI register for different classes by single application	Section 11(1), 84(1), Rule 23(3)
Part A of the GI register for different classes by single application	Section 11(3), Rule 23(5)
Part A of the register from a convention country for different classes by single application	Section 11(3), Rule 23(4)

Once the application is ready in all respects, it can be filed before the Registrar [26] of Geographical Indications for registration. After receiving the application, the Registrar shall examine the application in a pre-determined manner and may refuse the application or accept it absolutely or subject it to some amendments, modifications or conditions if any as he may deem fit as per the Act.

Under Section 12, when an application for registration of a geographical indication has been accepted and either:

1. The application has not been opposed or the time for notice of opposition has expired; or
2. The application has been opposed and the opposition has been decided in favour of the applicant;

The Registrar shall, unless the Central government otherwise directs, register the said geographical indication and the authorized user, if any mentioned in the application and the geographical indication and the authorized user it shall be registered as of the date of the making of the said application and the date shall be subject to the provisions of Section 84 and it shall be deemed to be the date of registration.

However, if the registration is not completed within twelve months from the date of the application by reason of default on the part of the applicant, the registrar may treat the application as abandoned. The registration of GI shall be for a period of ten years but may be renewed from time to time in accordance with the provision. However, the registered proprietor shall on application made in the prescribed format can apply for the renewal of the registration before the expiry of the registration period. In this case, the registrar can renew the registration of the product as per the provision of the Act.

Special Provision Relating to Trademarks and Prior Users under GI Act, 1999

With a view to avoid confusion relating to the use of trademark for the designated products, the Act has made special provisions in it. As stipulated, the registration of a trademark can be refused or invalidated which:

1. Contains or consists of a GI with respect to the goods or class or classes of goods not originating in the territory of a country, or a region or locality in that territory which

such GIs indicates, if use of such GIs in the trademark for such goods, is of such a nature as to confuse or mislead the persons as to the true place of origin of such goods or class or classes of goods;

2. Contains or consists of a GIs identifying goods or class or classes of goods notified under sub-section (2) of Section 22 of the Act. However, the trademark granted and subsisting before the GI Act came into force shall not be invalidated. As such the provision has tried to address the difference that exists between the designated GI and trademark.

Remedies on Infringement of Goods

During the time when India did not have a GI Act, the Indian judiciary played a significant role to protect GIs. It has applied the common law principle of passing off [27] as suited under the Indian conditions in case of GIs. Thus, the Indian courts had given effect to the provisions of Articles 22 and 23 of the TRIPS Agreement even before the GI Act was enacted in the country with the enactment of GI Act, 1999. The legal system for containing infringement has been further strengthened with the inclusion of both: (i) criminal remedies, and (ii) civil remedies for providing effective protection to the designated products.

Criminal Remedies

The GI Act, 1999 has included provisions for containment of infringement like:

1. Falsifying and falsely applying GIs to goods.
2. Selling goods to which false GIs is applied.
3. Falsely representing a GI as registered.
4. Improperly describing a place of business as connected with the GI registry.
5. Falsification of entries in the register.

The punishment prescribed for the aforesaid offences varies from six months to three years imprisonment or/and fine of not less than ₹ 50,000 but may extend to ₹ 2 lakh.

However, the court has been empowered by the Act for adequate and special reasons in writing off or imposing lesser punishment.

The Act also prescribes for enhanced penalty for second or subsequent conviction. The term of imprisonment in such cases shall not be less than one year but it may extend up to three years and fine of not less than ₹ 1 lakh, which may extend up to ₹ 2 lakh. The discretion is vested with the courts to impose a lesser punishment than the minimum punishment after recording the judgment for awarding lesser punishment. No cognizance would be taken of any conviction made before the commencement of this Act. The offence under the Act is cognizable. The Act empowers the court to direct the forfeiture to Government, of all goods and things by means of or in relation to which certain offences mentioned therein have been committed. The court may either order for the forfeited goods to be destroyed or otherwise disposed off. Further, the Act empowers the deputy superintendent of police to take cognizance of GI offences and may search and seize things and articles involved therein.

Civil Remedies on Infringement

The Act has also provided adequate provisions for initiating civil remedies for containment of infringement. However, the registered proprietor will have to take the initiatives for the purpose.

The suit for infringement has to be filed in court not inferior to that of a district court having jurisdiction over the area. If in any suit for infringement of GIs, the defendant pleads that registration of the GIs relating to plaintiff is invalid, the court trying the suit shall:

1. If any proceedings for rectification of the register to the GIs relating to plaintiff or defendant are pending before the registrar or the Appellate Board, stay the suit pending the final disposal of such proceedings;
2. If no such proceedings are pending and the court is

satisfied that the plea regarding the invalidity of the registration of the GIs relating to plaintiff or defendant is *prima facie* tenable, raise an issue regarding the same and adjourn the case for a period of three months from the date of the framing of the issue in order to enable the party concerned to apply to the Appellate Board for rectification of the register.

Effect of Registration in the Context of GI Act

The registration bestows the right to the proprietor [28] to exclude unauthorized users [29] from using the GI. Registration of GIs shall give to the registered proprietor and all authorized users whose name has been entered in the register, the right to obtain relief in respect of infringement of the GIs. However, authorized users alone shall have the right to use the GIs in relation to the goods in respect of which the GIs are registered. This right is subject to the conditions and limitation on which the registration is granted. Two or more authorized users of a registered GI shall have co-equal rights, which make the IPR different to the other form of intellectual properties.

Status of GI Registration in the World

Literally, the European Union played a leading role for inclusion of GI as an important instrument of IPR in TRIPS Agreement. The Union has also pioneered in implementing the GI Act for protecting the unique products of the EU member countries. As on 2010, about 10,300 products have been registered in the world under different country-specific GI Act out of which more than 58 percent belongs to European Union. Among the EU, 5.8 percent belongs to France followed by 4.2 percent of Italy and 1.3 percent of Spain. It is pertinent to mention that most of the products registered are agricultural products and a large chunk of the products belongs to wine, spirits and cheese of different member countries.

Status of GI in India

As of March 2013, 193 unique products have been registered at the GI Registry, Chennai. Though most of the registered GIs were of Indian origin, few products of other countries [30] have also been successfully registered in the national territory.

It is interesting to note that majority of the applications filed in 2012 in India are from the member countries of EU. One of the striking features of designated GIs is the diversity of products registered under the said Act.

It includes textiles, handicrafts, foodstuff, agriculture, beverages, and horticulture products. Amongst the 193 registered products, handicraft is leading the chart with 128 followed by agriculture (46) and manufactured (15). Handicraft also includes unique handcrafted textiles of the countries like Bhodoi carpet, Sanganeri print, Bagh print, Pashmina shawl and many more. Hence, if the handcrafted textiles are included in the textiles, the registration from the textiles and clothing will lead the table.

Notably, most of the products so far registered belong to traditional knowledge category and bears generational legacy as the making of these unique products have been passed on from generation to generation by the artisans and reflects the rich cultural heritage of the country. Further, the predominance of creative and agricultural products among the designated GIs clearly indicates that GI has a significant potential to facilitate rural development particularly, in the context of farmers and artisan communities and hence can be used as an effective instrument for rural development.

Even if the trend of registration and filing up of applications appears to be promising, [31] India is still far behind as compared to the other countries. As of 2010, the products registered in European Union under PG [32] PDO [33] and TSGs [34] were more than 5,000, whereas the number in India was just 169.

However, it is interesting to note that most of the products registered belonged to wine and spirits only in EU, whereas the Indian basket of GIs is more diverse and contains both agricultural, non-agricultural products and food stuffs.

In the Indian context, one of the important trend emerging since the enactment of the Act is the people's participation and stakeholders' response to the GI. It is evident that the application for 3 products was filed during 2004-05, which increased to 24 during 2005-06 and to 45 during 2008-09. As such, the total number of products registered during 2010-11 had increased to 169. It is evident that response of the people has increased over the period of time, which is definitely a promising proposition.

The contribution of the different sectors indicates that the important sectors, which are way ahead in the registration, are agriculture (26 percent), handicraft (28 percent) and textiles (24 percent). Further, if we include textile crafts to that of textile products, its share would be 37 percent, which is more than any other sector. It appears that the textile and clothing sector is more sensitised with respect to the IPR protection through GI than other sectors. One of the important components is that the inclusion of human skill as one uniqueness for GI registration might have helped tremendously for promotion of these products.

Further, the diverse socio-cultural ethos of the country has given rise to plethora of intricate and artistic hand-woven textiles in the country since times immemorial. The cultural integration of the traditional Indian culture with the Muslim invaders during the 15th and 16th century has brought about a series of socio-cultural changes in the country. It has also influenced the manufacturing sector of the country particularly the traditional labour intensive sectors like textiles, handicraft, leather and to some extent, agriculture. The cultural change during those decades gave rise to a series of intricate and cultural-oriented artistic hand-woven and hand crafted textile products. Further, the inclusion of western culture has also included some new dimensions to the intricacies and value addition to these products.

Hence, the producers require protection by earning their livelihood through the production and trading of these products. These products are also catering to a niche market and fetches premium price for the artisans. The large scale infringement of the products with replicated cheap and similar design products has also threatened the very existence of these products. At such a juncture, the GI registration can bring some solace to these culturally attributed products, which is continuously fighting for survival in the 21st century. Similarly, it may be the case with agriculture and other traditional knowledge products.

Conclusions

GIs are anchored in particular territories and they contribute to the social and economic dynamism of many regions across the world. They create local jobs and favour the diversity and originality in production. GIs allow producers to dedicate themselves to the marketing of typical products that meet consumer demand in terms of origin and quality. In addition to the above, GIs make value addition to the products besides contributing to the preservation of environment, natural resources as well as the protection of a culinary, artisan, cultural and often, the ancestral heritage. In India, most of the products, having geographical indication, belong to agriculture and textile sector. The role of these sectors in employment generation, reducing regional disparities, increasing per capita income has been enormous. The first product protected under GI registration in India is Darjeeling tea followed by 'Pochampally Ikat'. Since the country is bestowed with a large number of traditional knowledge and creative artistic works that are unique to a geographical region, protecting these products under geographical indication will help preserve them against poaching in the fiercely competitive world market.

Further, the empirical evidence of some of the products protected through GI has indicated that the protection is not only creating a mechanism for securing the product from unauthorised mass poaching but also brings about some positive changes in terms of price, quality and productivity. It also has a positive impact on the perceptions of the consumers.

The elimination of infringement also brings healthy competition and increases the premium price of the GI designated products.

Hence, countries should focus to register more and more such products under their respective GI acts.

End Notes

1. The multilateral treaties includes Lisbon Agreement, Paris convention etc.
2. Collective mark is a mark, whose use is permitted only to a collective body. The body can be an association or co-operative of manufacturers, producers or traders. The use of collective mark is governed by regulations which have to be submitted to the industrial property office together with an application.
3. Such authority may be local council or an association, which is not engaged in the production/trade of the product concerned.
4. Paris Convention was signed by 166 countries in 1883.
5. Madrid Convention was signed by 74 countries in 1891.
6. Lisbon Agreement was signed by 20 countries in 1958.
7. Revised in 1900, 1911, 1925, 1934, 1957, 1967 and amended in 1979 and the 1989 Madrid Protocol relating to that Agreement.
8. Revised in 1911, 1925, 1934 and 1958.
9. Lisbon Agreement was revised in 1967 and amended in 1979 and the 1976 Regulations under that Agreement were amended in 2002.
10. Part II, Section 3 of the TRIPS Agreement has explained geographical indications in detail.
11. Article 22.3 specifically elaborates with regards to the registration of trademarks, containing or consisting of GI.
12. Article 22.4 stipulates that the protection under Article

22.1 to 22.3 must also be made available in respect of the use of deceptive geographical indications, i.e. GI that is literally true, although they falsely represent to the public that the goods on which they are used originate in different territory.

13. Excerpts from TRIPS agreement on GI.
14. The term 'generic name' denotes the name of goods which, though relating to the place or the region where the goods were originally produced or manufactured, has lost its original meaning and has become the common name of such goods and serves as a designation for or indication of the kind, nature, type or other property or characteristic of the goods.
15. Article 24 of the TRIPS Agreement lists five exceptions.
16. Including the EU, Bulgaria, China, the Czech Republic, Hungary, Liechtenstein, Kenya, Mauritius, Nigeria, Pakistan, the Slovak Republic, Slovenia, Sri Lanka, Switzerland, Thailand and Turkey etc.
17. Such as India, Bulgaria, Czech Republic, EU, Hungary, Liechtenstein, Kenya, Pakistan, Slovenia, Sri Lanka, Switzerland, Thailand, Turkey etc.
18. Kerly defines 'passing off' as an actionable wrong for the defendant to represent, for trading purpose, that his goods are those or that his business is that of the plaintiffs. In *Consorizo de Proscuitto di Parma vs. Marks and Spencer*, Nource, L.J. also identified the ingredients of a passing off action as being comprised of three namely: (i) the good will of plaintiff; (ii) the misrepresentation made by the defendant; and (iii) consequential damage.
19. The Scotch Whisky Association, a company incorporated under the Companies Act of the United Kingdom.
20. The Scotch Whisky Association a company incorporated under the Companies Act of the United Kingdom, Pravara Sahar Karkhana Ltd., a manufacturer of various brands of Indian Whisky called Blended Scotch whisky or Blended with Scotch.

21. The Registrar of Trademark is the apex authority constituted by Government of India for registration of trademarks in the country.
22. Registrar of GI is appointed under sub-section (1) of Section (3) of the GI Act, 1999.
23. ₹ 5,000 for each class. The Act classifies the goods into different classes.
24. Both state and central government agencies.
25. The Indian action could be: (i) Indian Companies Act, (ii) Indian Society Act or any other Act deemed to be suitable for the purpose.
26. The Registrar of GI, Gunna Complex No.443/304, Anna Salai, Teynampet, Chennai-600 018.
27. The court have granted injunction restraining the defendants from advertising and offering for sale or distribution in any country goods (including wines and sprits) where they indulge in colourable imitation and unfair trading to reap harvest by exploiting the goodwill of any goods or products which is essentially attributable to specific geographical area and is used in relation to particular goods originating from any country, region or locality, as the case may be.
28. The producers' associations, consortiums who are registered in Part A of the GI Act, 1999.
29. The producers/traders, who are registered in the Part B of the GI Act, 1999.
30. 'Pisco' of 'Peru', 'Champagne' from France and 'Napa Valley' from the United States have been filed under the GI Act, 1999.
31. The total number of products registered is 149 while 236 applications have been filed before GI registry. The trend is increasing every year.
32. Protected geographical indication.
33. Protected designation of origin.
34. Traditional specialty guaranteed.

3

GIs as Instrument for Sustainable Development: A Case of Pochampally Ikat

Tapan Kumar Rout

Introduction

The economic rationale of IPR protection through GI is closely associated with the perception to link origin as a quality signal for marketing the goods for sustainable development of the producers' community. It protects the consumers from deception by eliminating quality-price disparity. The registration of the product under the GI Act provides an important legal tool to the proprietors to initiate infringement action against the unethical business practices through judiciary system. It also helps in realising tangible benefits for the stakeholders through systematic and sustained brand promotion and market linkage of the designated products in post-GI period. Most importantly, GI could be an instrument to curtail the market distortion arising out of information asymmetry between buyers and sellers. It can be viewed as a process, where reputation is institutionalised in order to solve the problem of information asymmetry and unethical free riding on goodwill associated with the products. The registration acts as a consumer protection measure and also at the same time protects the producers by safeguarding the reputation and quality of the product.

Empirical Evidence on GI Benefits

Researchers have made attempts to quantify the impact of the IPR protection of unique products and traditional knowledge (TK) through empirical research in order to quantify potential benefits of GI as an instrument for socio-economic development of the producers of the designated products. A consumer study organised by the EU Commission in 1999 has estimated that 40 percent of the consumers are willing to pay a premium of 10 percent for origin guaranteed products (EU Commission, 2003). The consumers' willingness to pay higher premium price for the original products may be attributed to the elimination of uncertainty on the quality and originality of product.

A study conducted by OECD highlights a number of factors that influence the small and rural enterprises dealing with unique products and penetrating the niche markets. The two important factors that have emerged are: (a) market access, and (b) market differentiation. One approach to address these factors could be to work collectively in order to develop a competitive advantage. The approach is well accommodated with an origin labelled validation strategy confirming the economic rationale for protecting geographical indication. It can also influence the rural economy as most of the origin-labelled products originated from rural areas.

On product specific studies, the Jamaica Bru Mount coffee received a premium of US$ 14.50 per kg. in comparison to benchmark prices of Columbia miles. The study of EU Commission has further highlighted that GI provides value addition to the producers by facilitating product diversification and maintaining specific quality standards. The French GI designated cheese is sold at a premium of 2 Euro per kg. over other non-protected cheese. Likewise, Italian Toscano Oil is sold at a premium of 20 percent, since it was registered as a GI in 1998. Further, many of these products whose names are protected have experienced enhanced exports during post-GI period. It has been estimated that 85 percent of French wine exports and 80 percent of EU exported spirits use GI's as a marketing tool for promoting the product both in domestic and export market. The GI has become a lifeline for 1,38,000 farms in France and 3,00,000 Italian employees during post-TRIPS period.

The studies on regional origins and prices of wine have also given rise to positive impact on GI registration of the products. The primary econometric tool used in the analysis is the hedonic pricing model on wine and it allows estimation of the value of such important features as a geographical origin, variety, vintage, etc. whose inclusion brings about an additional premium for the original products. Schamel and Anderson (2003) extended this analysis to the case of Australian wines and found that regional origin has become a more important determinant of prices over the period 1992-2000 as compared to other factors. Their study indicated that the average premium price of the product has increased by 31 percent in 2000 as compared to 1992 for select Australian wines. The Pinot Noir is cheaper by 22 percent compared to a Shiraz from the Barossa Valley, while a wine produced in Canberra is 25 percent more expensive than its counterparts. The difference may be attributed to the guarantee of the quality of the products through GI registration. The trends have pointed out that the products once registered can act as a riding force for free trade. Today, Italian producers are calling their "parama ham" as number one ham in Canada because of the protection of the product through GI act and its widespread appreciation and acceptance by the consumers in Canada. Broadly speaking, the IPR protection of unique products may give rise to the benefits as outlined in the following sections.

GI as a Means to Protect Traditional Knowledge: Designated GIs are being increasingly considered as an instrument for protecting the traditional knowledge (TK) of the indigenous people in a legitimate way. This component of the TRIPS Agreement includes both the socio-cultural aspects as well as the production process involved in the process of manufacturing the traditional knowledge.

In the process of production of "handicrafts", the technical content can be protected as a technical idea, while the cultural value as a form of expression and its distinct characteristics can be protected through the symbol of a mark or indications. Therefore, perhaps in the negotiating committee of the World Intellectual Property Organisation, while a few countries look at different IPRs for protecting traditional knowledge, most of the countries look favourably at GI as the best means for protecting traditional knowledge. It is because of the fact that GI as an instrument, possesses some specific characteristics than any other form of IPR and is hence considered relatively more suitable for the customary traditional knowledge of indigenous people. The suitability of GI for protecting the technical knowledge can be attributed to the involvement of community ownership for maintaining quality and goodwill of the products.

Community Ownership and Codification of Quality: This is the only form of IPR which stipulates community ownership, as most of these products are produced by a particular community. The exclusive monopoly of the ownership lies with the producers' community and hence, the fear of commodification of traditional knowledge on account of GIs does not apply. Protection gives rise to legal codification of the well established practices, which results in difficulties in infringement and mass poaching by unwanted and unethical business practices. In the present structure of globalisation, it may be difficult to safeguard these products unless and until a sustained way of protection is available and in this regards, GI could play a pivotal role.

The IPR protection through GI is closely related to the quality parameters of the products. A particular product is protected as long as the quality parameters prescribed in the registration are maintained. As such, the quality aspects of the product have to be identified and codified in the process of registering the products and can act as a catalyst for the development of the product in terms of enhancing marketability and creating confidence in the minds of consumers. The codification of the production process also helps the consumers from deception and helps producers for expanding the horizon of brand value of the product. The example of Darjeeling tea should find a mention in this context.

The aroma of Darjeeling tea can never be matched with its replica variants as the quality of this tea is ensured by the place where it is grown which is characterized by high altitude with corresponding geo-climatic conditions of Darjeeling which is unique. We can also consider *Khadi* products in this context to elaborate the importance of codification of quality. Though Khadi cannot be confined to a particular geographical location in India, in the context of GI, quality codification in terms of design, pattern, quality of raw materials, dyeing, weaving and finishing touches should lend ample credence to the cause of this important product. The GI tag should not only ensure that Khadi is commanding a premium price, also it is effectively combating the low cost-lesser quality dubious variants which are unethically flooding to the market to exploit market sentiments.

Protection for Socio-cultural and Traditional Rights: This is with respect to collective rights provided by GI, open to all producers in a particular region. Unlike other IPRs, the rights cannot be licensed by the manufacturers or its associates based outside the purview of registered geographical area, which is not a case for trademarks or patents. Hence, the cultural ethos and traditional knowledge involved in the process of production of these unique products are preserved. At the same time, it is the only IPR, which is free from any adverse socio-economic results of corporate control and accumulation that occurs in other forms of rights. Even if this right provides a collective monopoly to the community as a whole for using it as an instrument for commodification and the brand building of the product, it does not create a monopolistic structure in the market segments.

Therefore, GI remains meaningful in enabling people to translate their long-standing, collective and patrimonial knowledge into livelihood and income. The example of *Khandua* pata is worth mentioning here to illustrate the importance of empowering traditional rights. Historically, this product can be traced to the days of great poet Jayadev, when entire *Gita Govinda,* the famous work dedicated to the Lord was weaved on a Khandua pata and was presented to Lord Jagannatha. Since then, Khandua patas are worn by Lord Jagannath and has its popularity in the state of Odisha till today. The GI protection will ensure that the socio-cultural and traditional rights of the weaver community are not neglected and they get a premium for the products. This will ensure sustainable livelihood for many entrepreneur families with expertise to produce high quality traditional clothes and staves off competition from unethical sources.

GI and Information Asymmetry: In economies, this form of IPR plays a crucial role by helping the consumers to distinguish the products coming from specific regions to that of other regions. It safeguards the expectations of the consumers by distinguishing the unique product category. In other words, GI brings about product differentiation by minimizing the role of market failure called information asymmetry, where it can be described as a situation in which consumers are unable to observe all the characteristics relevant to a good i.e. taste, quality etc.

A relevant classification of goods into three categories on the basis of the degree of information available to consumers while purchasing can be articulated here in the context of GI. In the case of *search* goods like garments, quality can be ascertained by consumers before purchase. In many cases, the qualities of the products become known after purchasing and using the same. The example is the quality (taste) of a food brought from a restaurant. These are called *experience* goods. For other goods, certain quality aspects are rarely learned even after consumption e.g. toothpaste. These goods are called *credence* goods. In the case of credence goods, the information asymmetry is acute and brings about confusion in the minds of the consumers for which government intervention is often required to reach acceptable supply of product quality.

If consumers cannot distinguish the quality of different product varieties before purchasing, they may be reluctant to pay different prices for the products that look alike. For example, in case of red wine, all products looks similar and the consumers do not have the reasons to expect that one variety of wine is more qualitative than others. In these circumstances, instead of thinking about the quality aspects and the originality, the consumers may prefer to go for the cheaper one. This may be a case for all original products. In these circumstances, GI can serve as an instrument for product differentiation and facilitate a desirable level of premium price for original and unique products.

Protection against Free Ride by Third Parties: When a product is registered under the GI Act, it prevents unauthorized producers from using the designated GI and thus protects it from free riding on reputation of the authentic produce, that have been produced over a period of time. The guarantee that products carry, confirms originality and origin from a specific area also conveys information on certain product characteristics to the consumers. Production in the respective region may lead to specific qualities that are essentially attributable to geographical origin, for instance, in relation to climatic factors. But it may be the case that the intervention of individual producers from the area has an additional impact on the characteristics of the final product. For example, the specific method used to transform silk into special weave as in case of Banaras Brocades sarees of India.

Further, regional producers sharing a distinctive signature product need to agree on certain characteristics of the final product or the production techniques to be used if the signature product is to remain relevant to consumers. Given that, typically, more than one producer has the right to use the same GI, the potential of free riding also exists within the relevant producer group. It can be addressed through registration, where producers' association, for instance, are able to find a way to ensure that the significance of GI is not ruined by the opportunistic behaviour of individual members. The producers through co-ordinated approach can also maintain quality of the product. As a result, the economy as a whole benefits from higher product quality and a larger product variety.

GI as a Stimulating Factor for Price: It is believed that the products protected under GI Act or contemporary Acts are fetching higher premium price as compared to similar products which are not registered. Some studies have even indicated that the consumers are willing to pay higher premium for the GI designated products than others because of the elimination of uncertainty on the quality and origin of the product. The consumers are assured that these products come from the right region with desired qualities.

Schamel and Anderson (2003), in their study, analysed the case of Australian wines and found that regional origin was an important determinant of prices over a period of time (1992-2000), with average premia of up to 31 percent which the Australian wine commanded in the year 2000.

GI as a Facilitator of Free Trade: The trends of some GI designated products points out that the products once registered can act as a riding force for free trade. Today, Italian producers are calling their "parama ham" as number one ham in Canada because of the protection of the product through GI act and its widespread appreciation by the consumers in Canada.

GIs as an Instrument for Rural Development: Most of the designated products and traditional knowledge of different countries are closely associated with rural areas. The products also have a close affinity to socio-cultural ethos of the producers' community. These unique products having originated from a particular territory are one of the most important manifestations of regional identity which can be considered as a useful instrument for economic development of the producers' community and preserving the local tradition and culture. The effectiveness of GI as a tool for rural development in developing countries could be more prominent, as the designated products could enter the niche and lucrative markets of both developed and developing countries to fetch higher premium price for the producer community. The success of GI as a developmental tool, however, depends on exogenous factors like the nature and quality of the product, characteristics of production process, uniqueness and the marketing channels. If these parameters relating to the products are well integrated with the IPR protection through GI, the designated products could effectively serve the purpose and facilitate rural development.

However, the assessment of the developmental impact should not be limited to the standard criteria (high prices, increased sales, rise in employment and income). Instead the distribution of the benefits within the rural areas, the level of participation of local actors, reproduction of social system and environmental impact are the factors which should be taken into account to ensure sustainability.

A Case of Pochampally Ikat

It is imperative that IPR protection through GI provides much needed protection against infringement and helps the consumers from deception besides promoting economic prosperity of the producer community. The most important benefit from GI is that it reduces, if not completely, eliminates unfair competition, which ultimately benefits both genuine producers and consumers. In order to protect the traditional knowledge from infringement and ensure the development of producers, the weavers of Pochampally Ikat registered their hand woven textiles under the GI Act of India in the year 2004.

Protection of Market through GI: The Pochampally Ikat was registered under the Geographical Indication Act during the month of November 2004. It is presumed that the parameters of market, the supply chain and the organisation of the manufacturing have undergone changes over the years. Given this scenario, our attempt is to map the growth trajectory of successful handloom enterprises and locate them in the context of the growth of the handloom industry of Pochampally. The study will also examine the comparative market position of pre- and post-registration periods, which will document and provide a platform for comparisons. A protected product under GI will have a quality of its own to maintain its reputation, and hence, the consumers of the product will benefit from purchasing quality products. Since, the opening of the market has been effective from 1st January 2005 and registration of unique products of textiles and clothing under GI has taken up more recently, this study make an attempt to examine the implications of GI registrations for the manufacturers of Pochampally IKat.

Market Analysis of Pre- and Post-GI Registration Periods: Pochampally hand-woven textile weaving centre in the state of Andhra Pradesh in India is known for famous hand-woven silk and cotton saris, ladies dress materials, furnishings, etc. over the last 200 years. The Ikat textile is woven by using tie and dye techniques of yarn, which is the specialty of the centre. In this process, wherever colour is not required in the yarn, the yarn bundles are tied with rubber strips before undergoing the process of dyeing. Two different processes like vat and napthol dyeing are used in the dying process as per the requirement. The products are produced in the traditional pit looms and the products bear a legacy for generations.

Around 5,000 artisan households work in the centre—the Ikat weaving is a way of life and source of their livelihood. This unique product experienced many difficulties during last 50 years due to widespread infringement by the large mills. The marketability of the product reduced due to availability of cheap infringed products in the market, which gave rise to reduced demand for the original product. The decline in demand of the products resulted in low income for these artisan families and subsequently most of them diverted to other occupations bringing the product to the stage of near-extinction. In such a situation, the enactment of GI Act of India provided a platform to this unique craft for protection. Subsequently, the artisans successfully registered the product in 2004 under the Geographical Indication (GI) Act, 1999 of India.

It is believed that with the IPR protection of the product, the demand for Ikat has increased and so also the other key variables like price, productivity, employment and the overall income of the artisan households. In order to quantify the benefits of the protection to the product and the producers, a study on comparative market analysis of pre- and post-GI registration period was conducted. The result of the study gives a promising picture to the product as a whole. The analysis of the data collected from a sample of 256 small and medium enterprises (SMEs) out of 3,000 enterprises, the co-operative societies and the producers and trading associations during the pre- and post-registration period has indicated that the key variables of the product like price, quality, productivity, employment, and the income of the producer has increased in the post-registration period.

The producers have also undertaken product diversification in the post-IPR protection period so as to cater to the growing demand of the consumers. However, it is also noted that the structure of the industry though has changed drastically in the post-GI period; the size structure does not seem to have changed radically. It may be noted that the change in the size structure will need large investments, the entry of new artisans joining the industry and the extent of perceived demand for the Ikat will play its role in the mindsets of these cottage-industry manufacturers.

Moreover, the trend of the key variables has given rise to a new hope for this unique textile, which has experienced a decline in production during the last decade of 20th century and early years of the 21st century because of large scale infringement by the mills and other manufacturers.

The key trends explained in Table 3.1 indicates that the production of the selected samples have increased from ₹ 11.94 crore in 2004 to ₹ 22.94 crore in 2009, indicating a growth of more than 14 percent from the year of protection. It is important to mention that prior to protection the turnover had a negative growth due to declined demand, leading to low income of the artisans. It also induced the skilled and unskilled artisans to divert to other economic activities like agriculture, rickshaw pulling, etc. As such, the registration has brought about a turnaround in the production activities of this famous craft, which is definitely an important experience for the producers.

Table 3.1: Trends in Key Indicators of the Products (Production, Productivity and Employment)

Parameters	Year						Growth Rate
	2004	2005	2006	2007	2008	2009	
Production (value) (₹ crore)	11.98	12.89	13.27	15.93	19.12	22.94	14.09
Employment (Number)	452	456	464	614	619	628	8.46
Productivity (in mtr)	190.53	210.54	217.22	238.94	262.83	289.11	8.47
Sales Turnover (₹ crore)	9.61	11.44	11.68	14.37	17.68	21.74	17.33

Similarly, the employment for the sample enterprises has also grown by about 8.46 percent over a period of 6 years in the post-IPR protection period, which appears to have a demonstrative effect on the economic activities of the region. It may be because of the various factors—like the exodus of the working population from this part of the rural India has been minimized due to the economic prosperity of the artisans associated with the product. Similarly, the economic activities of the area other than agriculture has increased, which could have a important spillover effect on the area as a whole in terms of increased activities on retailing, support services to the product like dyeing, finishing and packaging activities, etc. One of the import findings of the study was the enhanced productivity during the post-registration period.

The productivity also experienced more than 9 percent growth in the post-IPR protection period. In hand-woven textiles, the productivity is generally low due to intricacies involved in the process of production. The designs and intensevity of the work further makes the process more complicated and hence low productivity. However, the increased demand for Ikat products due to protection, branding and other related activities might have provided rich dividends to the artisans in terms of higher motivation and enhanced income, which ultimately may have brought about a rise in productivity. No doubt, the trend could be an eye opener for the thousands of unique textile producers across the country.

The most famous product of the Pochampally Ikat is Pochampally Saree and Telia Rumal. Even if the centre is famous as a silk production centre, of late, the artisans have also tried to weave cotton sarees, home furnishings, ladies dress materials etc. to cater to the ever increasing demand for these products. It is evident that the process of product diversification and so also the trend from silk to other fibre products accelerated during the post-IPR period, the artisans have resorted to product diversifications and weaved ladies dress materials, home furnishing like bed cover, curtains, pillow covers, bedspreads, wall hanging, etc. These products have also attracted both the domestic and overseas buyers. As such, the price of the products in the post-registration period has also experienced a robust growth, as shown in Table 3.2.

The price of the silk saree, one of the traditional products of the centre has increased by more than 17 percent during the period, where as the price of diversified products like ladies dress material and fabrics has increased by about 13 percent. The post-registration period has also given rise to a big boost to the production activities of the centre. As such, the positive effect of GI registration is clearly visible in the trends of the key economic parameters of the production centre.

Table 3.2: Trends in the Prices of the Products

Products	2004	2005	2006	2007	2008	2009	Growth Rate
Silk Saree (₹/pc.)	1,443	1,505	1,600	2,000	2,500	3,125	17.38
Cotton Saree (₹/pc.)	360	380	380	456	547	656	12.99
Cotton LDM (₹/pc.)	233	236	242	291	349	419	12.99
Cotton Fabrics (₹/mtr.)	66	68	68	81	97	117	12.62
All	1,405	1,466	1,558	1,946	2,431	3,037	17.33

Conclusion

The paper has tried to analyse the economic rationale for protecting geographical indication in the context of a theoretical framework. The theoretical explanation is further validated by a case study of a registered product called Pochampally Ikat. It is evident that providing protection for the designated products through GI is more than just monopolization; rather the economic rationale is based on the consideration of the value addition and market differentiator that arises from the IPR. It is pertinent that the protection of unique products can give rise to sustainable development of the products if and when the protection is effectively converted to tangible benefits for the stakeholder's thorough brand promotion and market linkage. In case of Pochampally Ikat of India, the producers have already experienced the developmental angle of the GI as they are able to harvest the tangible benefits in terms of enhanced premium price and rise in employment. However, from the policy perspective, much empirical studies need to be taken up to quantify the direct and indirect implication of geographical indication, particularly with reference to the developing countries.

4

GIs and Socio-economic Development

T.N. Singh

Introduction

Indian economy is always boosting up due to development in use of basic raw materials available in the surroundings. An emerging and fast growing economical expansion is an edge over other countries because of cost effective and labour intensive economical base/cost in India.

It is a well known fact that the knowledge available in a society, community and country is a treasure for development from social and economic point of view. Sometimes, these developments have created conflicts among many groups, regions and countries. These conflicts germinated to law for protection and promotion of the idea, which can later be converted into the process and product. These have given the idea of patent, trademark, copyright etc. However, there was no law for protection of origin of goods—regards its location, process and local climatic condition—which plays a crucial and critical role and makes the product of international reputation.

The product may be of a high commercial value—may not be today—but there is always a scope for refinement and up gradation of the product to make it marketable. The classical examples are 'Champagne of France', world famous 'Feta cheese from Greece' whose tradition dates back to thousands of years, tea produced in Darjeeling area, Banarasi silk and sarees, Kolhapuri sandles etc. These products have something in common through their generic names and reputation. However, these types of products are produced and marketed in other places also but that does not meet the quality, reputation and tests due to change in climatic conditions or particular skills of the people involved.

To avoid such situation of clash and long legal battle, geographical indication came into the existence as intellectual property laws (IPRs) in the TRIPS Agreement of the WTO, which came into force in 1995. It is further defined in Article 22(1) of TRIPS agreement as an indication, which identifies a good as originating in a particular territory, community skill or a locality in that territory, where a given quality and reputation or other characteristics of the good is essentially attributable to its geographical origin. Indian government enacted this Act in 1999 and enforced it w.e.f 15th September 2003, through Ministry of Commerce, Government of India under the patent, copyright and geographical indication (GI) section. GI registry is based in Chennai office of IPR in Tamil Nadu state.

The Act is unique in different ways and means due to its broad spectrum. A special symbol/sign is used which indicates the origin from a specific geographical region, unique process and strong and deep reputation. In majority of the cases, the geographical name associated with the product instills the faith and belief of consumer regards its originality. Sometimes, the local climatic conditions with unique soil features or physical or chemical characteristics control the quality and test which cannot be duplicated in any other environment in a changed geographical location.

In case of India, there is need for popularization and awareness of this program due to low level of education and rural base of the population. Greater awareness would not only help the people to understand about GI use, but would also improve the number of products from different regions and localities which have not made a global impact yet. Many of the local products are not known at the national level, being popular only at the local level. This may be due to lack of facilities or lack of awareness which makes the product confined to a particular area. The process will certainly improve the quality of life of people in the area, in terms of economic upliftment and expansion of the product base.

In India, there is a wide scope and application of GI but due to poor documentation habit, many of the processes has been confined to a family tradition, particularly traditional knowledge transferred through verbal communication from generation to generation. Many a times, we have paid a heavy price for this as is in the case of basmati, turmeric etc. It is well exposed, particularly in tribal areas where education is at a low level. There is an urgent need to document this unique treasurer for protection and its prevention from misuse at national and international level.

To register a GI product in India, the applicant must have an Indian address with serving in the country. It can be applied by an individual on behalf of a society, community or group of people of that region where the product production and process lies. Once the application is received at the office, it will be scrutinized and examined by the experts in the area (GI Booklet, 2007) and if any drawback is noticed, within a month, it can be rectified, upgraded or modified to prove the correctness of the product/s.

Once this process is over, GI registry may ask for queries from the applicant and the report is prepared within two months with full satisfaction and reviewed by an expert panel to verify the supporting documents for it correctness. If the application is found correct, then it will be published in the National Journal of the Ministry for public awareness and comments. If any party/group is affected due to the applicant, they can appeal to registry for hearing, with proper supporting documents. If there is no opposition, then a certificate will be issued by the registry in this regards.

So for, more than 160 products of different categories have been registered successfully. These products are mainly from agriculture, textiles, handicrafts, foodstuffs etc. The first GI was approved way back in 2004 for Darjeeling tea under 'goods' as per Section 2(f) of the GI Act, 1999.

Flowchart of a GI Application

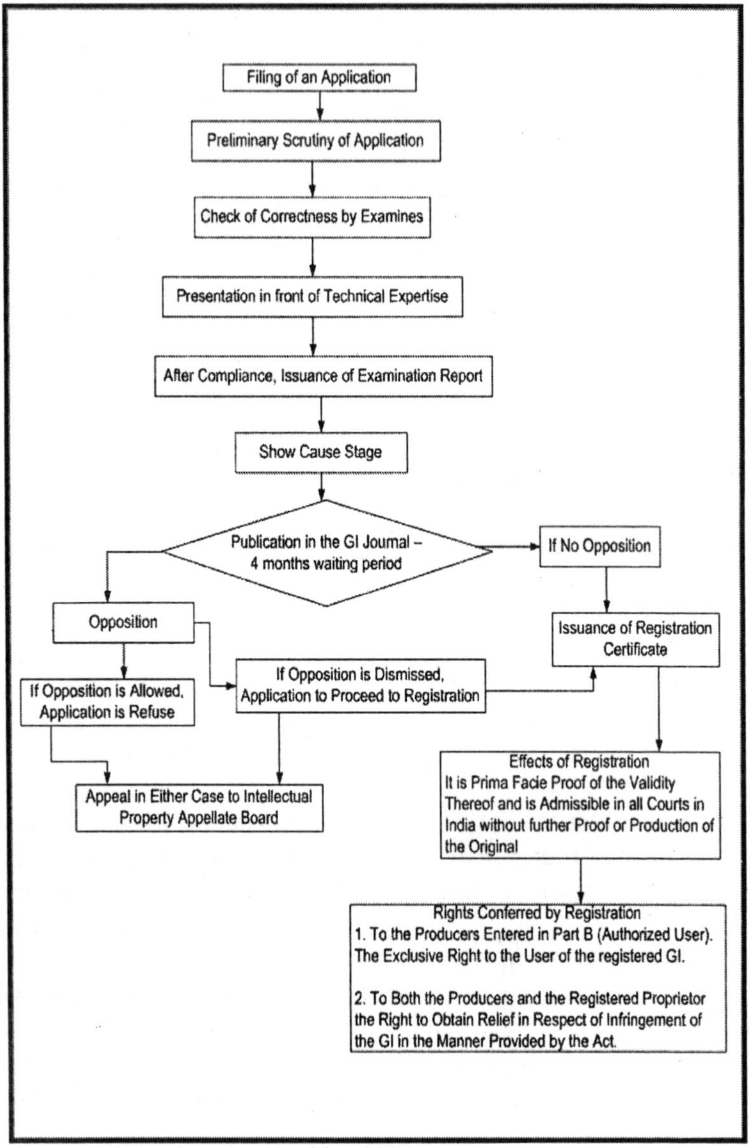

Source: GI Registration Booklet, 2007.

Need of GI

GI is indeed required because of duplication, dishonest approach and the wrong supply of goods to consumers at the cost of real price. This deteriorates quality, reputation of the product and economical loss to the real producer. The fake and dishonesty sometimes cause a conflict between two regions, communities and countries. GI is essentially the soul of nature impregnated into mother Earth and hard to fully clone it. GI is very well and widely connected to tradition, culture and heritage and confined to specific geo-boundaries.

Hence, the GI protection should not be confined to only commercial value of the product but also for the preservation and protection of tradition and cultural knowledge. It is one of the alternative tools for:

1. Maintaining local harmony due to sole participation in the process.
2. Valuing the heritage and cultural aspect.
3. Protecting and promoting traditional knowledge to make it an economical backbone.
4. Valuing agro-ecological characteristics and geo-friendly growth of the region.

GI for Social Cause

No society can grow unidirectional. For an all round progress, participation of every individual and feeling of belongingness is the key to growth, which will be long lasting, stable as well as sustainable. A defective growth cannot bring harmony and happiness for any society. GI provides reputation with respect to territory and interest of producers.

Social development is a key for good governance and GI is a value addition for sustainable growth. The scope of GI is enormous, particularly in the Indian prospective because of enormous resources that have not been completely explored because of wider diversity of climatic conditions. GI can be considered similar to trademarks in the sense that GI can act as a function of source indicator. GI is more close to environment because it is not putting resources under stress or work under diversity but harmony to the nature and society. It has been a tried and tested method from generations to generations. It can encourage and put development with systematic dynamism, renewal of resources and aesthetics.

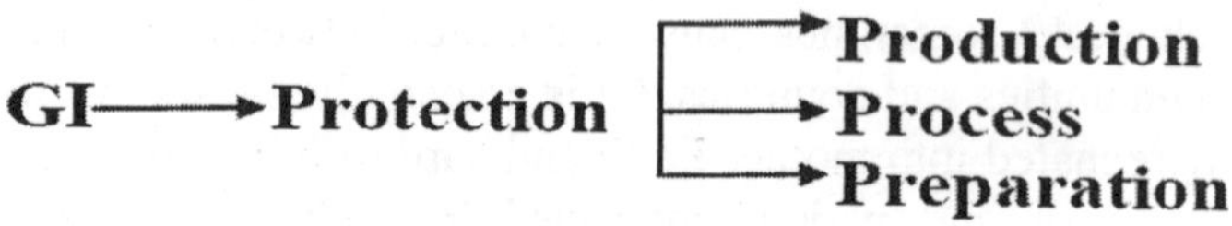

GI can help to improve and promote the following:

Flow Diagram of Social Development

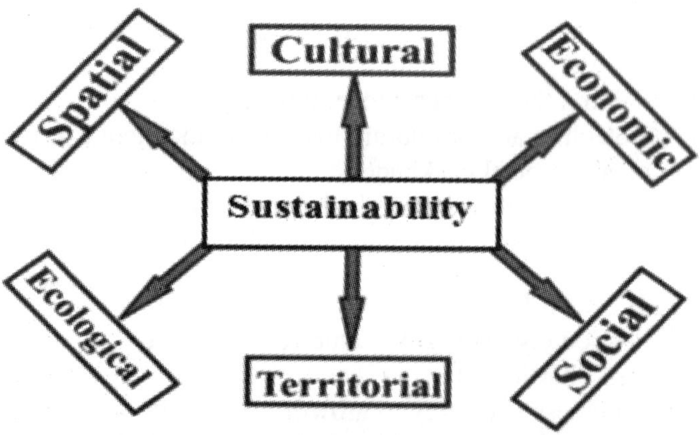

Growth through GI

Faster growth is taking place in urban areas due to maximum exploitation of resource availability, which is the root cause of migration—whatever limited resources are available are not ready to cope up with such a huge pressure. The imbalance initiates conflict like social, cultural, and economical. To prevent such migration, a designated plan of action is required at various locations to provide better essential services. This will not only help to protect the indigenous knowledge, which is priceless but also balance the growth and population pressure. Once, the local knowledge base (LKB) migrates, then there are possibilities of extinction of the existing knowledge. Then, by no effort, we can bring back the value and knowledge treasure which has been lost. Thus, it is pertinent to provide in rural areas, good economic governance through GI.

There are many success stories outside India about GI, which has brought economical growth with a systematic marketing strategy but in India, we have to act fast and promote the GI products in an aggressive way to provide better and actual price of the products to the real producers. Most of the GI products have an impact on market and are acceptable in nature due to its broad value, based on conservation effect and technological response like Banarsi Sarees, Chanderi silk, Mysore silk, Lucknow cotton, Agra petha etc.

Sometimes, human skill is more valuable than any technological skill and bamboo and craft work of North Eastern part of India is a classic example where people can make amazing products through their understanding and imagination. The craft work is now well received outside the North Eastern part and is a good economical source for the people who are involved in the process. There are also well established cottage industries in the North Eastern part of India.

There is no doubt that GI is an indicator for growth and prosperity but there is a need for greater efforts to manage the people, taking the local talent and skill into action mode. The future challenges are to make systematic and scientific documentation of fragmented knowledge base available at various corners which are specific, unique and reputed. There is a need to manage the resources based on qualities, reputation and goodwill of the products.

GI can provide both long-term as well as short-term benefits to producers and consumers, but it requires:

1. Valuable marketing tools in global economics,
2. Maintenance of quality,

3. Better legal protection,
4. Better control over duplication and fake marketing, and
5. Better quality at affordable cost.

It is also necessary to reduce the conflicts among the people having diverse views due to the cooperative working system for a common goal, which may further minimize social conflicts. This may enhance rural development, minimize migration and improve human development index through social and economic strengthening.

GI is not about protecting the interests only of an individual but also protecting the interests of regional communities or groups who are the real producers. The benefit goes to the authentic creator and not to the middle men. The economic development through GI will be for the place and people who can bring sustainable development

Geographical indications can endorse the economic growth in various ways for the society and the community. Indian economy and the market mainly functions on four models. The functional work is given below:

1. Rural products-Rural consumers (R_P-R_C).
2. Rural products-Urban consumers (R_P-U_C).
3. Urban products-Rural consumers (U_P-R_C).
4. Urban products-Urban consumers (U_P-U_C).

GI takes mostly the first three options and has a massive market potential. India has approximately 17 percent of the world's population and 0.6 percent share in world trade and 1.4 percent share in world GDP. It has an ample and demanding market for GI products not only within India but outside India also. A huge market is available for cotton products, tea, craft and silk items as well as food products. The scope of food products and textiles is very promising.

GI-A Value Addition

India has peculiar human skills (tools and techniques). These skills have been tried, tested and verified for a long period. Some products have historical background and good impact which will facilitate their promotion in the market.

Some of the traditional and local knowledge products/tools are still better than the modern technology e.g., tin processing by tribals in Bastar District of Chhattisgarh from Cassiterite ore with local skills having better purity than our known mineral processing which is complex and expensive in nature. Adoption of such local technology can reduce the cost of production and enhance the purity and consumption of even low grade ores, which are locally available in plenty. If this technique is fully functional, then low grade ores, which is a waste material today can be economical due to high price in world market with cheaper, effective and efficient technology. Particularly, tin ore availability is limited in India and requires adoption of such local tools and techniques to enhance the recovery.

GI Inter-relation With Surroundings

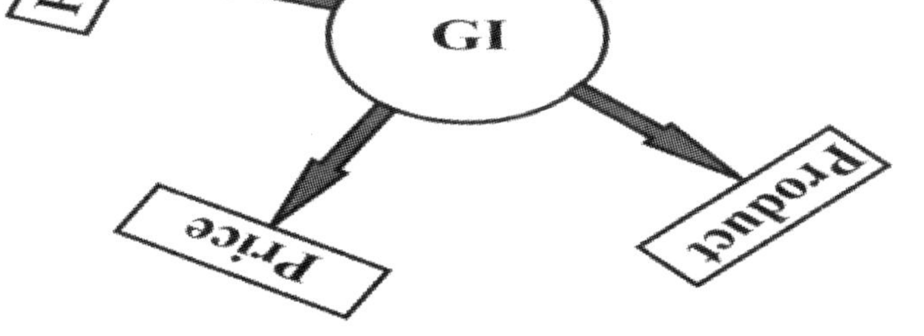

Tribals from Jharkhand near Ranchi produce different varieties of iron from low to high grade iron ore, which has more than 95 percent purity using local techniques and skills. We are not in a position to process low grade iron ore and most of the ore is sold to China or Japan. There are many more such examples like, Goa Feni, Lonawala Chiki which are produced locally but having a global outreach. There are plenty of Indian products waiting for GI protection to boost the economic conditions of the real producers and not the middle men. The role of various government departments is crucial for protection, promotion and prevention from misuse of the GI tool up to a greater extent. It is one of the best tools to minimize poverty from the rural areas. There is a need for policy shift to improve the marketing of GI through cooperative societies, tie-up with big shopping complexes, on-line marketing etc.

Concluding Remarks

Geographical indication is a multi-dimensional phenomenon which can enhance the social, economic and cultural heritage of India and bring back its glory globally. It will help to develop systematic and scientific approach to protect the rights of the people who are custodians of a particular GI product. There is a further need to make it more popular and government should take it as a mission project. Good vision, wise mission and prompt action are the keys to success for GIs. GI is one of the prudent ways for long and safe protection of traditional knowledge, its flavour and fabric which has an immense potential for the growth of the heritage and cultural treasure bestowed on us.

5

Building Brands through GIs

Anuradha Maheshwari

Introduction

The saga of human evolution is replete with major and minor developmental milestones, social, political, economic and environmental; not the least being the marked genetic mutations reflected in man's physique and features proclaiming his geographical ancestry and habitat. The ethnicity of the people, including the arts, crafts, goods and trade coming from the region are unmistakably stamped with the distinctive style and attributes of their geographic origin, so much so that the goods, like the inhabitants acquire a reputation linked to the region.

In fact, historical accounts, stories, fables and folklore abound in references to myriad products that have been uniquely distinctive and are the proud hallmarks of the region in which they are produced like the *Mughal meena bazaar*, *Mathura's dairy products* or the *Greek feta cheese (made traditionally in Greece from ewe's milk and finds mention in Homer's Odyssey)*. In each case, a geographic name became associated, far beyond the borders of that geographic location with a product known for highly desirable and seemingly unique characteristics and with further passage of time got linked with certain skills, know-how, processes that could not be replicated independent of the region. Consequently, a certain value, a price tag got attached to these products, that became a harbinger of the growth and well-being of that region and nation.

The 14th and 15th century medieval Europe saw a surge in the development of regional trade linked to the promotion of local arts and crafts and process know-how through a system of rewards and monopolies. The monopolies were granted to a community of artisans and individuals as creators and as beacons of standards of the representative quality of artefacts coming from a region. Against this backdrop, we find the genesis of the development of the modern day international intellectual property law system, in particular through the promotion of the beautiful and stunning "Venetian Glass" art form, then prevalent in Venice, Italy.

Geographical Indications

As property in intellectual creations gained recognition as a right of the creator, geographical indications seeped into the arena of intellectual property to be protected as a much needed boost to international trade. Though initially, at the time of the Paris Convention 1883, they were recognized as 'appellations of origin' and 'indications of source'; today, they have acquired an individual identity and are one of the prime revenue builders for a nation. As mentioned in the TRIPS (Trade Related Aspects of Intellectual Property Rights) they are known as geographical indications, and are defined as 'any indication, name or geographical name, figurative representation, expression conveying territorial origin or source of goods and refers to the protection of only those products originating from a certain geographical area. The TRIPS Agreement of 1995 is said to be the first multilateral treaty dealing with the term 'geographical indications'.

The term includes any direct or indirect reference to the geographical source, characteristic or qualities of a product. In an effort to protect geographical names, three concepts were developed, from the most all-encompassing to the most specific: indication of source, geographical indication and appellation of origin. All appellations of origin are geographical indications and all GIs are indications of sources. An appellation of origin must necessarily indicate specific qualities, reputation or other characteristics essentially or exclusively attributable to the geography of production, like *Nagpur oranges, Darjeeling tea, Sheffield cutlery etc.* Names like basmati rice or a feta cheese however, unlike appellations of origin would be mere geographical indicators of products but without the attachment of geographic names.

While the politics of GIs are intriguing, at heart the debate about geographical indications is a struggle about commercial linguistics, myth maintenance, and who will extract the monopoly rents from those myths. This is what makes the geographical indications debate, both so interesting and so parallel to conventional trademark law. Though like the trademark the distinctive function of a GI is to link the product and services to its origin and help identify the producer or artist who made the product, the overall advantages of a geographical indication far outweigh that of the former.

Club Goods

As opposed to the private monopoly right of a trademark, GIs create public community rights benefiting a larger group collectively and sidesteps the threat of unfair monopolistic trade practices. Registered GI products typically function like 'club goods' and do not belong to the realm of any one producer to be exploited by him exclusively. On the contrary, it is a right to be collectively exploited by the community of craftsmen etc. involved in the production of the goods, stimulating thereby a healthy competition *inter se*, and generating a set of non-rivalrous rights that do not diminish one producer's right over another. Typically, they articulate the obligations that must be complied with by all the users of a given indication and set out the rights to be protected against third parties.

These rights enjoy a far broader scope of protection primarily because they cannot be assigned or exhausted like other intellectual property rights; in the sense that they cannot be further sold or licensed commercially. The most fascinating attribute of geographical indications is that they though they function like a trademark; the rights remain with the community in perpetuity (to be renewed periodically), while the knowledge underlying their status remains in the public domain. They perpetually benefit an entire community of producers, stimulate the economic growth of the region and the country and most importantly protect goods that are already famous. In fact, a geographical indication status pre-supposes the existence of a certain reputation already enjoyed by the products and services they seek to protect legally.

However, it must be borne in mind that their specificity and distinctiveness is essentially born out of the territory of the produce, from the unique geographical characteristics such as soil, climate and traditional skills like process know-how, craft etc. At issue is whether a product with essentially similar characteristics can be produced in a different physical/human environment or not. It must be recognized therefore, that GIs require more than the mere protection of *geographical names* because of the triple association always between the product, its place of origin and quality related factors. Also, consumer acknowledgement/acceptance plays an important role in determining the eligibility of a product as a geographical indication. To qualify for legal protection, it is necessary that the name and reputation of the particular product has been established by pre-existing trade.

GIs and Consumer Protection

Once protected, a geographical indication has multiple advantages—it protects the interests of honest producers and traders, generally the economically backward traditional craftsmen by preventing unfair competition, cartelization, and commercial abuses, specifically unauthorized use. Through the creation of internal competition and fair play, protected geographical designations help to improve not only the quality and reputation of products in the domestic market but ensure a wider product access and greater prosperity through their exports into international domains.

More importantly, geographical indications effectively serve as a guarantee and assurance of authentic quality products, thereby minimizing consumer deception. In the battle for monopolistic conquests, the welfare of the consumers is usually overshadowed by the ambitions of the producers. The aspirations to supersede one another, leaves the consumer faced with the quandary of having to choose between varieties of products of barely acceptable quality. They not only have to overcome the issues of quality delivery, but also have to worry about the originality of the product. The promise of GI for the consumer in fact stretches from the seal of origin guaranteeing the source to the quality indicators that point to goods with a definite history and traditional knowledge evoking a certain aura, mystique and exoticness associated with the locale.

A key factor in the growth of brands and their legal regulation is the separation between the consumer and producer. In the last century, this distancing process accelerated rapidly for manufactured goods, but less for agricultural goods. Now, however, with modern packaging, transport and global trade, the separation between consumer and producer has rapidly increased in agriculture too. In such circumstances, registered GIs are one method by which a small-scale producer, far away geographically from the consumer, can reach through to that consumer with a consistent quality message.

GI registered goods are a huge draw with consumers also because of the traceability factor (of the raw materials) and that it gives them the flexibility to develop preferences especially for the palate (aroma and appearances included with respect to food products, like say a *basmati rice over surti kolam or a Dehradun basmati over an Amrisari, a Kashmiri Zafran over Spanish or a Cabernet over a Chardonnay (wines).*

Goods assume value linked to the perceived exoticness of the locality of production, uniqueness of product and it being not commonly available like a commodity. In various studies conducted across Europe, some interesting consumer behaviours came to light, chief among them being that consumers were willing to pay a premium price for GI products as follows:

1. 40 percent of European consumers were ready to pay a 10 percent premium price for GI products-*EC Study 1999,* on tea and champagne.
2. 75 percent of Italian consumers were ready to pay a 20 percent premium price-*Etude Nomisma Qualivita de '03.*
3. In case of special and unique geographical attributes, as in the case of specialty salts, gourmet cooks are willing to pay US$ 80 a pound for such varieties versus 30 cents for common table salt, for e.g. the Indian black salt, Portuguese Algarve salt, Australian Murray River Pink Flake salt, II Buco Handcrafter Italian Wooden Sea Salt, French Fleur De Sel and Clay-tinged red Alaea Hawaiian Sea Salt-*Business Week, 2004.*
4. History and tradition associated with production process command a higher price and value, like in the case of Parmesan cheese and Parma ham. Parmesan cheese is one of the oldest Italian cheese developed about 2,000 years ago in the castled city of Parma, Italy, the same place which is credited with the delicious Parma ham. It is the culinary tradition of that location that has enabled it to build its reputation.
5. Mystique elements like process secrets with legends and folkore, intrigue the consumers more than the regular products in the market place, e.g. Parma ham.

GIs and Brand Development

What is observed in the context of the above is that in the clamour for the protection of a geographical indication, one is in essence protecting a community intellectual property and quite often a domestic or international brand. For example, *Darjeeling Tea, Basmati Rice* is a brand both in India and abroad, which explains why the Government and the local producers both want to protect them fiercely for fear of infringement or dilution of the brand. Brand names allow producers to achieve market recognition, differentiate their offerings and gain legal protection not to mention the revenues they enhance through premium pricing of their products.

However, the power of branding has eluded producers of commoditized products for long. A promising new development is the recent use of geographical origin as a basis for branding commodities. That explains why a *Moet* or *Chandon* are so sought after as champagnes. A study of GIs reveals how diligently and consciously producers and governments are toiling to develop their products into brands and how building an image of quality leads to quick consumer acceptance that generates special value both for the producers and the consumers. A case in point would be the promotion of Colombian coffee and Havana cigars as one of the world's best coffee and cigar brands.

Colombian Coffee

Till 1959, public perception of the best coffee producer was Brazil. Colombia received almost no mention although it produced 12 percent of the world's coffee and was second to Brazil. The National Federation of Coffee Growers of Consumers undertook the branding exercise of their rich home-grown coffee through the use of a character named Juan Valdez and his mule, and used the catch line—"Buy Colombian when buying Coffee". They went on to promote it as the "richest coffee in the world" and used other tag lines like "50 percent tax bracket 100 percent Colombian coffee"- "No Colombian, no thank you".

The campaign succeeded and was quite fruitful in securing them as one of the leading coffee producers. By 1980s, awareness about Colombian coffee reached 96 percent, where 62 percent believed Colombia grows the best coffee and were willing to pay a 15 percent premium on Colombian coffee. The marketing strategy of the FNC resulted in an increase from 9.1

million USD to 13.2 million USD in revenue earnings.

Havanas

Likewise, Cuba fought hard and long to save its world famous brand of 'Habanos'—the premium quality cigars more commonly referred to as Havanas.

Their origin can be traced to 1492 when Columbus arrived on the shores of Cuba and their quality can be attributed to the geo-climatic conditions of Cuba and a clever blending of five different varieties of tobacco leaves to produce the variant in the market place.

However, over a period of time Habanos became a generic term to designate high quality cigars from all cigar producers in the world threatening the Cuban cigar industry and market. Eventually, the Cuban authorities took drastic steps to control the damage to the geographical name and along with various lawsuits, signing several bilateral agreements with other cigar producing and marketing countries, developed a marketing strategy in the 1980s to support and complement the protection efforts.

The first step was to establish a communication strategy based on the Habano appellation of origin. And the second started in 1991 by unifying the various versions of the logo and design for Habano that existed in other languages and using just one: Habanos.

From then on, the Habanos logo has the same image all over the world and the Habano Cuban cigar trademark printed on the boxes of brand names is the guarantee that these cigars are backed by the Habano 'Denomination of Origin' protection. This is a guarantee of quality and origin that is awarded to only the best cigars manufactured in Cuba under the strictest quality control measures, with the best leaves selected from the island's tobacco regions.

One can appreciate then that a mere registration of a GI as such does not guarantee returns for either the community of producers or the economy itself. In order to facilitate consumer awareness and investment returns, it is essential to build this pseudo-trademark into a brand and maintain it at that. Some regions have become synonymous with high quality products like Champagne in France, Cuban Habanos, Darjeeling tea, Basmati rice, Swiss watches, knives and chocolates; Japanese electronics, German automobiles and the likes.

Which is why post-2000, India as a WTO member and a TRIPS signatory has woken up to the merits of GI protection for an agro-based traditionally rich country like ours. Apart from enacting the Geographical Indications Act, 2000, it is actively encouraging local producers of famous indigenous products to protect them though a process of registration at the Geographical Indications registry office based in Chennai. Today, we can boast of more than 200 applications and 120 registered GIs strengthening the implications of GI policies, both nationally and internationally. While the most fundamental benefits of GI registration for producers is to cash in on the reputation theory, the actual profitability of the product crucially depends on the size of the market for these products. Without a sizable international market, a GI label and its expected price premium would fall short of the costs needed to be incurred to continue with the production, establishing the need to focus on building strong GI brands through unique and distinctive marks. Among the existing Indian GIs, Darjeeling tea and Basmati rice are the front runners in terms of international market and exportability.

Indian Success at Brand Building: Darjeeling Tea

The first attempt on the part of the Tea Board of India (which was constituted in 1954 under the Tea Act of 1953), towards protection of the 'Darjeeling' brand was undertaken way back in 1983, with the creation of the 'Darjeeling' logo. The Tea Board then obtained domestic protection for the Darjeeling logo as a 'certification trademark' under the Indian Trade and Merchandise Marks Act, 1958 (now the Trade Marks Act, 1999). In the same year, the logo was registered as a trademark in several other countries like UK, the USA, Canada, Japan, Egypt, Germany, Austria, Spain, France, Portugal, Italy and Switzerland. Today, it is a protected mark in 21 destinations with three more pending. In the absence of a separate law dedicated exclusively to GI's in India during that time, the word 'Darjeeling' was also registered as a trademark. When the Geographical Indication Act in India was enacted in September 2003, the Tea Board applied for GI protection of 'Darjeeling' in October 2003 and in 2004 became the first application to be registered in India as a GI.

Further, in order to prevent the misuse of 'Darjeeling' and the logo, the Tea Board has since 1998 hired the services of *Compumark*, a World Wide Watch agency which monitors and reports all cases of unauthorized use and attempted registration of the name and logo. From 1998 to 2002, the Board spent an equivalent of USD 2,00,000 to protect against infringement. International disputes relating to Darjeeling tea have been settled through negotiations undertaken by the Tea Board of India with the foreign companies. For example, Bulgari, Switzerland agreed to withdraw the legend 'Darjeeling Tea fragrance for men' pursuant to legal notice and negotiations by the Tea Board. Almost 15 cases in the last four years against infringement and misuse of the word Darjeeling Tea worldwide have been fought against countries like Russia, USA, Japan, France, Germany, Israel, Norway and Sri Lanka etc.

The quality, reputation and characteristics of Darjeeling tea are essentially attributable to its geographical origin. It possesses a flavour and quality which sets it apart from other teas, giving it the stature of a fine vintage tea. As a result, it has won the patronage and recognition of discerning consumers worldwide for more than a century. Today, as one of India's premier GI brands, production yields have also increased in its 86 tea gardens from 545 kgs./hectare in 2003 to 650 kgs./ha in 2005 producing approximately 10 million kgs. of tea. Incidentally, the activity has also played a major role in the empowerment of women of that region as nearly 50 percent of the labourers in the tea gardens are women. Consequently, Darjeeling tea that is worthy of its name cannot be grown or manufactured anywhere else in the world.

Dilution

However, when a geographical name becomes a generic term for similar kinds of products or the same product being produced in a different geography, the brand of the GI is said to be diluted. The exotic appeal of the product is lost and the product reputation suffers, becoming tarnished or blurred, leading to the genericide of the brand. This is a common marketplace phenomenon and normally occurs when popular geographic designators are used by many, to the extent of registering them as trademarks.

Pepsi Snacks attempted to usurp and register a geographical name 'Bikaneri Bhujia' (actually produced by hundreds of small producers) as a trademark in order to capitalize on the known geographic association and market appeal of the food product and was forced to withdraw the application. In similar instances, we find the Champagne brand being protected through a fierce watch against infringement worldwide, while the Scotch Whisky Association in the UK takes offenders passing off the 'scotch' name to court, as they have done with Khoday Distilleries (Peter Scot case) and Pravar Sahakara (Indian Whisky-Scottish drumbeater wearing kilt) in India.

Brand dilution also leads to commoditization of products and jeopardizes the interests of local artisans and craftsmen who lose out in the marketplace along with the consumers who cannot ascertain the origin of the commoditised products. For example, the famous Persian carpets are being imitated and produced by carpet weavers outside Persia, leading to confusion about their source and authenticity. The same is true of restaurants claiming to be Italian and beers claiming to be German.

Dilution Cases

Basmati Rice: This particular strain of rice is naturally grown in the northern part of India and south eastern parts of Pakistan and is a much in demand premium quality aromatic rice. However, there have been various imitations and modifications in many countries pertaining to the name Basmati, wherein rice was sold as Texmati, Calmati, Kasmati, etc. Due to this, the Government of India has fought over 100 trademark cases in over 30 countries over the term Basmati.

Darjeeling Tea: Though the actual production capacity is 10 million kg., 40 million kg. is sold worldwide. This happens due to most of the production from Sri Lanka and Kenya (Pure Darjeeling).

The Parma Ham case is not only illustrative of the dangers of dilution of geographical brands but also serves as an outstanding example of maintaining a supply chain integrity, that helps protects and creates valuable geographical indicators. Asda, a UK supermarket owned by Wal-Mart was recently taken to court by the Consorzio del Prosciutto di Parma and Salumificio, the Italian Parma Ham Trade Consortium, claiming dilution of the Parma ham brand. They alleged that Asda sold the product sliced and pre-packaged in the UK, whereas the reputation of the brand and the protected designation was not merely based on the place of production but also on how thin the slices were and the way it was packed. The genuine way to slice it, as claimed by the Consorzio was to make sure it was done in Parma at the plants in the designated areas, approved by organization responsible for monitoring Parma ham production. On an appeal to the House of Lords, Asda was restrained from the retail sale of Parma ham which had not been sliced, packaged, and labelled in accordance with the laid down specifications.

Conclusion

As mentioned earlier, mere registration of a geographical indication does not ensure its visibility in the market place. Consumers also ought to be made aware of the prominent position enjoyed by GI products in the market place with their registration, necessitating thus, intellectual property awareness as well as information on GI products. The encouragement of GI registration should also be accelerated, along with aggressive promotional campaigns.

This article would be incomplete without due reference to the critical socio-economic developmental role that GI brands play in the progress and advancement of a community. It is now apparent that promotion of geographical products is bound to result in industrialization and standardization of production processes as is seen in the case of products like wine, ham, cheese etc. as opposed to home-made, backyard processes. So, without compromising on traditions, a greater degree of uniformity and mechanization of production processes have crept in. Geographical identities are increasingly recognized as a tool that farming communities could use effectively to add value to agricultural produce, improve brand recognition and protect their product against competitors.

Considering that GIs generally draw upon products such as agriculture, fisheries, handicrafts and artisanal products, any trade advantage obtained from the GI status is basically pro-poor. This is in contrast with the other forms of intellectual property rights such as patents and trademarks where the gainers are mostly rich people (ICTSD 2004). Due to the community benefit endowed upon, the producers of a geographical indication, most obviously would ensue a competition for premier position within the community itself, stimulating further growth and development and a regular income flow in exchange of the guarantees it offers.

In India, the development role of GIs is amply illustrated through the examples of Moradabad brass workers and the 'bidri' workers of Karnataka.

Bidri in India is an 800 year old art form from the Bahamani kingdom influenced by Persian artisans who had migrated to the kingdom from Persia. Its specialty lies in the detailed ornate patterns made of zinc and copper, with silver inlay work. The lustre of the artefacts is due to the sand sourced from the fort of Bidar. The priceless labour involved, was however, unorganized for many years and left the skilled artisans at the mercy of the exploitative middlemen and highly impoverished.

NABARD in 2002 started the cluster development program by setting up a Bidri colony in the district of Bidar, Karnataka. This eventually led to the formulation of a self-help artisans group. The Karnataka Handicrafts Development Corporation secured the GI tag in 2008 for the whole scale of activities there, improving consequently the lot of the artisans as also helping preserve the traditional knowledge and local know-how. And of course, one needs to emphasize how the entire protection process also encouraged diversification of production and scaled up the demand for the products both in the domestic and international markets.

Geographical indicators therefore, are often looked upon as ideal intellectual property rights due to their fundamental characteristics of benefiting multiple entities and various stakeholders involved in the promotion of a product, such as the producers/organizations, Government, local communities and regions in a collective and proactive way. The role they play in taking a nation forward both socially and economically, thus cannot be ignored.

References

Champagne, Feta, and Bourbon: The Spirited Debate about Geographical Indications, Justin Hughes, *Hastings Journal,* Volume 58.

Emerging Issues for Geographical Indications-Branding Strategies: by Sanjeev Agarwal and Michael J Baroney, *MATRIC Research Paper 05,* MRP9, January 2005, (dilution- basmati/Darjeeling).

Geographical Indications-The Experience of Indian Tea Producers: Protection of Darjeeling Tea, Naba Kumar Das, Chairman Tea Board of India.

Geographical Indications-A Search for Identity: Latha R. Nair and Rajendra Kumar.

Geographical Indications: An Opportunity for Japanese Speciality Quality Products, Tokyo, Osaka, Paul Vandoren, 10th-12th March, 2004, Anuradha Maheshwari, IIPS.

Geographical indications: Creation and Distribution of Economic Value in Developing Countries, Sophie Revron, NCCR Trade Regulation, Working Paper No. 2009/14.

Geographical Indications: The Parma Ham Case, Lee Adayachee, *Researcher,* Tralac.

Intellectual Property Organisation and the State Administration for Industry and Commerce (SAIC) of the People's Republic of China, 2007, Paper on GIs and Trademarks, Adargelio Garrido de la Grana, SA, Havana.

Protecting Geographical indications as Collective Trademarks: The Prospects and Pitfalls, Dev Ganjee.

Protection of Geographical Indications in India-Case Study on Darjeeling Tea, Sudhir Ravindran and Arya Mathew.

Quibbling Siblings: Conflicts between Trademarks and Geographical Indications, Dev Ganjee, LSE, (2007) 82, Chicago, *Kent Law Review.*

Socio-economics of Geographical Indications, Dwijen Rangnekar, www.ictsd.org/September 2004, No. 8.

Vadis, G.E. Evans and Michael Blackeney, *Journal of International Economic Law,* 9(3), 574-614, Advance Access Publication, July 2006.

What Determines the Price of Wine? AIC Issues Brief 18, University of California, Bombrun, Helene, and Daniel A. Sumner, 2003.

What's in a Champagne that aint in a Basmati?, Vishvas Deavaiah.

Whither Science in India: B.K. Sen, Commentary, *Current Science,* Vol. 92, No. 2, 25th January 2007.

WTO/TRIPS Council: March 2002, Statement by Switzerland on issues related to the extension of the protection of GIs provided for in Article 23 to products other than wines and spirits.

6

Integrating GIs with Development

Debdatta Pal and Amlan Das

Introduction

Over time, geographical indication (GI) has evolved as one of the most important intellectual property right (IPR) tool in India. GI is a unique category of intellectual property rights with collective ownership and links a product with its place of origin. The WTO Agreement on Trade Related Aspects of Intellectual Property Rights (TRIPS) defines geographical indications as follows:

"Geographical indications are indications which identify a good as originating in the territory of a country, or a region or locality in that territory, where a given quality, reputation or other characteristic of the good is essentially attributable to its geographical origin". (WTO/TRIPs Article 22.1)

A place-related name often indicates relevant information regarding quality as well as characteristics of a product (WIPO, 2006). Examples to quote: Bordeaux wine, Scotch whisky, Havana cigars and Darjeeling tea. The quality and characteristics of the product are exclusively or essentially derived from the geographical environment, including natural and human factors (Hopperger, 2000; Escudero, 2001). A geographical indication is considered as a significant indication of intellectual property as it identifies goods (agricultural goods, natural goods or manufactured goods) as originating or manufactured in a particular geographical location where the given quality or other characteristics is attributable to that location. For manufacturing goods to become eligible for GI, at least a part of production process has to be undertaken in the particular territory, region or locality. For example, while raw material (i.e., wool or silk) for 'Tangaliya' is procured from Ahmedabad, production takes place only in Surendranagar district in Gujarat state.

It been surfaced widely in recent IPR literatures (see Gopalakrishnan, et al., 2007; Gupta, 2008; Das, 2010) that GI has a potential to bring significant change in a region's economic performance through providing legal protection to the identity of indigenous products. Researchers (Suratno, 2004; Josling, 2005) have also looked into the legal or procedural aspects of product registration process. This paper attempts to contribute to this wide body of literature by assessing the impact of post-GI scenario of two handloom products from India. Taking GI as 'treatment', the article primarily revolves around a broad research question—'how promising are the post-GI socio-economic conditions?'. The justification for selecting product from the same sector lies in bringing synergy in analysis. Rationale for single country study is drawn upon the assumption that both the cases selected are exposed to similar country-specific conditions.

Theoretical Background

From a theoretical perspective, it is better to understand geographical indications in terms of economics of information and transaction cost. Information asymmetry between buyer and seller occasionally results into 'adverse selection' where low-quality products push high-quality products out of the market (Akerlof, 1970). The particular market failure calls for market intervention either from the trade bodies promoting fair trade or, through Government action to ensure flow of more accurate information across parties. This would one way help customers to make informed choices, and on the other, to hold repute of the particular product. In this regard, a geographical indication can be viewed as a signal of assured quality and would bring down degree of information asymmetry to a large extent (Josling, et al., 2004).

There is a need for mechanism which would significantly

lower the transaction cost, both ex-ante and ex-post among the stake holders to drive equitable benefits (Jena and Grote, 2007; Gupta, 2008). To quote Gupta (2008), 'Ex-ante transaction costs have four components: (i) searching information, (ii) finding supplier, (iii) negotiating contract, and (iv) drawing up the contract. The ex-post transaction costs include: (i) monitoring and compliance, (ii) side payments, i.e., concessions which can make the contract enforceable through modified inducements/discounts, (iii) resolution of conflicts if any, and (iv) redrawing the contract if none of the above helps in going ahead with the contract.'

Knowledge has the potential to be produced and further reproduced both culturally as well as socially and also through individual innovations (Gupta, 1999). Innovations flow through generations and generations and become an integral part of traditional wisdom (Gupta, 1980; Richards, 1985). But the holder of traditional knowledge may not be aware how the knowledge is unique and how it would derive greater monetary benefit. Upon identifying importance of the traditional knowledge, the knowledge holder would try to find out potential client of such information. Localized nature of knowledge and in cases knowledge been possessed by marginal section of community, make the search process very costly. On the other hand, searching cost for corporations and R&D institutions have also become significantly higher to find out the information holder.

After establishing the link between interested parties, next step lies in negotiating the best mutually beneficial deal. Unless potential value of the information is known to the knowledge holder, it is not possible to negotiate. Also, collective bargaining would benefit the whole community. Upon negotiating the deal, parties need to draw contract explicitly to ensure benefit distribution as per the deal. Reaching at terms of agreement acceptable by the whole community as well as to the other party is a complex issue. This involves high cost and resources. Inability to draw a right contract may yield asymmetric benefit and loose enforcement. Post deal challenges include enforcement cost to be borne by an economically deprived population.

This may not only result in inequitable distribution of benefit, it may even lead to erosion of knowledge source. Thus, upfront payment becomes inevitable for conservation of knowledge as the poor community is so vulnerable that it cannot wait for benefits to accrue (Gupta, 1999). Even after every due care the deal may not yield fruitful result and may lead to litigation and redrawing of contract involving considerable cost. GI to a large extent helps reducing these transaction costs. The registration of GI with the authorized body would act as a platform of information source to the interested parties. This would reduce information asymmetry about the product. Also knowledge holder could be reached easily by the interested parties.

Collective ownership of GI would help the knowledge holder to bargain at collective strength and bring benefit to the community. As registration with GI Registration body is a legal procedure, the process would make the community or, at least the body representing the community familiar with legal procedure. In this process, the community also becomes familiar with legal professionals. This would help to face any litigation or, redrawing of contract in worst case. Also to note that collective ownership of GI would bring necessary strength as well as incentive for ex-post monitoring.

It has been long advocated (see Gupta, 1994, 2003) that benefit of knowledge must be shared by its conservator. Products protected under GI have the potential to fetch benefit to knowledge holder which would incentivize the conservator for conserving the biodiversity and traditional knowledge (Bérard and Marchenay, 2008). While GI could act as a signal to differentiate the product and create a market niche (Das, 2010) it would also act as a legal tool to protect brand and prevent piracy (Correa, 2002).

Registration as Geographical Indication

The idea of GI could be traced back to the seventeenth century among European countries (Suh and MacPherson, 2007). European countries were eager to have a mechanism which could provide a protection to products attributed to certain origin (ORIGIN, 2005). The first international convention on geographical indication was the Paris Convention for the Protection of Industrial Property (1883), which was followed by the Madrid Agreement for the Repression of False or Deceptive Indications of Source on Goods (1891) and the Lisbon Agreement for the Protection of Appellations of Origin and their International Registration (1958). The WTO/TRIPS of 1995 was the first Agreement on geographical indications which is considered to have 'binding' effect. Due to the voluntary nature of participation in earlier conventions on GI, the scope of legal enforcement on non- participating parties was difficult. Contrary to this, WTO/TRIPS assured binding legal effect on all 149 WTO member countries (Baeumer, 1999; Babcock and Clemens, 2004).

Although from India around 1,500 products have the potential to qualify as geographical indicators (Natarajan, 2008), the initiatives were taken only in recent times. India brought a *sui generis* system of GI with enactment of the Geographical Indications of Goods (Registration and Protection) Act, 1999 (GI Act), coupled with the Geographical Indications of Goods (Registration and Protection) Rules, 2002 (GI Rules). Prior to this, the recourse of protecting any GI was solely lying with either through passing of judgment by court under the consumer protection act or through trademarks (Das, 2006). While a trademark is a sign used by an enterprise to distinguish its goods and services from those of other enterprises, a GI conveys the message to the consumers that the product is produced in a particular place and bears certain characteristics attributable to the place of production. Presently, Geographical Indications Registry at its office in Chennai enjoy the all-India jurisdiction with regards to GI. The procedure of GI registration is provided in Annexure I.

Cases of Geographical Indication in Handloom Sector

Indian handloom sector representing the rich socio-cultural heritage and carrier of a wide body of traditional wisdom continues to be one of the largest employers in non-farm sector with reported involvement of 6.5 million [1] people. The highly decentralized and dispersed nature of handloom sector can be observed in presence of over 400 [2] weaver clusters across the country. The sector is highly skill based with least technological intervention. But the widely dispersed nature as well as poor economic conditions of majority of the weavers has put the sector into the hands of master weavers where majority of poor weavers act as contract manufacturer of master weavers. In the process, lion's share of profit is taken away by master weavers.

The observed lower producer's share in consumer's rupee has attracted schematic intervention by Government through state agencies and cooperatives. But the emerging post-WTO scenario may bring down the scope of providing subsidy to the sector. This pushes the need to formulate strategies which would involve higher stake holder cooperation to ensure a win-win situation. In a recent market driven intervention, Ministry of Textiles, Government of India through Integrated Handlooms Cluster Development Programme (IHCDP) has attempted to support sustainable development of identified handloom clusters.

The programme is targeted to bring desired self-sustaining change through product development, capacity building, and establishing forward and backward linkage. Effort has also been taken to identify handloom products with potential for getting registered under GI.

Up to March 2013, the number of products which have got registered under GI has reached 193 (Table 6.1). Majority of them belong to the handicrafts category and amongst them maximum products are from the handloom sector.

Table 6.1: Status of Product-wise Distribution of GI in India up to March 2013

S. No.	Product Category	No. of Registered GIs
1.	Handicraft	128
2.	Agricultural	46
3.	Manufactured	15
4.	Foodstuff	4
	Total	193

Source: GI Registry, Chennai, India (accessed on September 13, 2013).

As may be observed from Table 6.1, out of 193 registered GIs, 128 (i.e. 66 percent) is handicrafts which include textiles, painting and other artisanal products. Traditional knowledge base of Indian handicraft primarily flows from generation to generation. This holds the risk of erosion of knowledge if it is not awarded properly for holding, creation and recreation of knowledge.

GIs have significant roles to play to bring home the benefit of trade. Efforts have been directed from Ministry of Textiles and Ministry of Rural Development, Government of India through cluster development programme to arrest the declining trend in handloom sector.

'Pochampally Ikat' is the first handloom product from India to get the rare distinction of being registered under GI Act in December 2004. This is an outcome of effort under Cluster Development Programme (CDP) to augment producers' share in consumer's rupee considering the vulnerable condition of the majority of weavers where 50 percent weavers were in the category of below poverty line. The effort was to provide a sustainable livelihood for the poor weavers who on one hand, were dictated by the unfavourable terms and conditions of the master weavers, and on the other hand, were facing competition from power loom made imitations. Textile Committee (2007) report noted that the clusters used to suffer from low productivity of traditional pit looms, near-stagnancy of skills, and dearth of innovation in design and product diversification as well as inefficient marketing efforts.

The exploitation was to the extent that while each 'Pochampally Ikat' silk *saree* (a strip of unstitched cloth of few metres in length which is draped over the body mainly by women) would fetch market price between ₹ 1,500 to ₹ 2,500 (Textiles Committee, 2007, p. 47), the wage rate was confined to ₹ 1,500 to ₹ 2,500 for a set of eight *sarees* (Textiles Committee, 2007, p. 20). The Report also highlights about the subsistence living of the weaver families on an average annual income of ₹ 8,000 to ₹ 10,000 which would make them vulnerable to any shock. The least bargaining power would result into distress selling of the produce. This is in one way helpful to avoid cumulative interest and on the other, to continue with the profession (Textiles Committee, 2007, p. 26).

As the registered proprietor of a GI in India has to be an 'association of persons or of producers', the Textiles Committee, in collaboration with a few other organizations, facilitated the GI registration of 'Pochampally Ikat' in the names of 'Pochampally Handloom Weavers' Co-operative Society Limited' and 'Pochampally Handloom Tie and Dye Manufacturers' Association'. The media coverage attracted for GI registration even helped to liquidate the piling stocks with increased demand experienced by the product. 'Pochampally Ikat' *sarees* witnessed an increased in demand by 15-20 percent (Chari, 2008 as cited in Das, 2010). Textiles Committee (2007) report indicates that year-on-year growth of sales turnover for 2005-06 reached 14.31 percent as against 12.01 percent in the previous year. Productivity growth for the corresponding periods stood at 5.88 percent and 4.35 percent respectively. This was associated with an increase in monthly income of the weavers.

Case of Tangaliya Shawl

In 2009, 'Tangaliya Shawl' made an entry to the prestigious league of few other handicrafts of Gujarat which were registered under GI—others being Sankheda furniture, agate of Cambay, and Kutch embroidery. The effort dates back to 2005 when 'Tangaliya' was taken up as one of the products for cluster development under Swarna Jayanti Gram Swarojgar Yajona (SGSY), an initiative by the Ministry of Rural Development, Government of India and National Institute of Fashion Technology (NIFT), Gandhinagar as the implementing agency.

'Tangaliya' is produced in Surendranagar district of Gujarat; the producer of the handicraft—a particular community called 'Dangasia' was spread over 26 villages in Surendranagar. This community was earlier a part of 'Bharwards'—the shepherd community. This indigenous craft has deep rooted origin and history of around 700 years embedded in the Saurashtra region of Gujarat. As per the legend, a 'Bharwards' man married a woman from the weaver community braving opposition from both the communities and settled on the outskirts bordering villages of both the communities. The offsprings born to this couple were later known as 'Dangasia' and had taken up the occupation of weaving. It was this new community that evolved this exquisite technique of weaving using yarn made of the raw wool that came from the sheep of 'Bharwads', who happened to be the shepherd community. 'Bharwards' are still known for their traditional profession as shepherds. The weaving technique initiated by the new community, 'Dangasia' was named as 'Tangaliya'. Presently, the 'Dangasia' community is known as the wool-weaving community of Gujarat.

'Tangaliya' has been, over the years, manufactured for the self-consumption of the producer community. 'Tangaliya' is traditionally a 10x4 feet cloth which is draped around the waist. However, because of the loom size constraints, the cloth is woven as 20x2 feet cloth and then cut into two parts and joined together to form a 10x4 feet cloth. The uniqueness of 'Tangaliya' is the beadwork, commonly known as *Dana* [3] that is used for designing different motifs. There are different types of 'Tangaliya' based on their colour and motif. 'Ramraj' print has high density of bright coloured *Dana* against black background with maroon horizontal lines. 'Charmalia' style has white *Dana* planted on black and maroon base colour. 'Dhunslu' style which has less *Dana* is mainly developed by aged woman. 'Lobdi' is used as head covering with white *Dana* against maroon background. Weaving of 'Tangaliya' is a household activity. It is woven on a pit loom which is generally installed at the weaver's home. The production of 'Tangaliya' is very complex and labour intensive. The expertise of weaver decides quality of the final product.

Weaving of 'Tangaliya' was for self-sufficiency and sustainability in supporting the entire community with the clothing according to climatic conditions and contemporary cultural needs. Due to self-consumption nature, this either remained unnoticed or beyond the reach of craft historians. Lack of exposure and non-viability of activity in its existing form had resulted into majority of weavers plunging below the poverty line. This has further pushed poor artisans to leave weaving and take up other professions like wage labour, leading to the possibility of the extinction of this traditional knowledge.

However, in spite of being a unique product which is produced exclusively in this area, the art faced several challenges over the years and faced extinction towards the start of this century. Reasons for poor condition of the art and its artisans are as follows:

1. **Narrow Product Line:** The product line was limited to only *shawl* that was mostly used by the local women to drape around their waist. Without any product variety, the market size was small and not sufficient to support all the families dependent on the art.
2. **No Buyer Power:** Artisans were buying raw material mostly from Ahmedabad city on individual basis at retail price. As a result, the buyer power was very low and they had to pay a high price for procuring raw material. To get

a reasonable margin out of the business, there was a need to push the price of final product upwards. But poor demand led to sale the products at a discounted price which narrowed the profit margin.

3. **Repetitive Design:** Placing of *Dana* in different patterns provides uniqueness to 'Tangaliya'. However, the weavers were using only some basic and restricted motifs in their product. The design was limited to basic patterns like flower, tree, house, star etc. or some geometrical structures like circle, triangle, square etc. Without a variety of designs, they were unable to attract new generation customers.
4. **Poor Marketing Ability:** There was no sales and marketing strategy for the product. Hardly people outside the region were aware about 'Tangaliya'. The producers were unable to reach out to the larger market for lack of market information and financial means.

It was becoming increasingly difficult for the artisan families to survive with meagre income generated by practicing this art. Many of them were forced to change their profession and started working as daily labourers. The future of 'Tangaliya' craft looked really bleak with no ray of hope.

It was in early 2005 when NIFT, Gandhinagar selected 'Tangaliya' as one of the five crafts for cluster development as a special project under SGSY—others being Khadi, single ikkat, brassware and stoneware. Objective was to build recognition for the distinctive art of poor artisans through promotion of clusters and helping them to generate income on sustainable basis. The cluster development initiative of NIFT, Gandhinagar was intended to create long-term self-employment opportunities for several rural marginalized artisans of Surendranagar district.

As the knowledge was traditionally used to produce woollen garments only for community consumption, it was understood that scale could not be attended with the existing products or with traditional design. The need was not only to save this handloom product from extinction but also to provide a platform and create awareness so that there would be a demand for the product in the market. The cluster development project aimed to meet its desired objective through innovative design, product line extension, skill development, technological upgradation, trend forecast, market intelligence, development of common facility centre, formation of self-help groups for both backward and forward linkages with markets and establishment of credit linkage with financial institutions for sustainable income generation. Intervention of NIFD was instrumental in developing the following areas:

1. **Sensitizing the Target Group:** As the SGSY scheme emphasizes on group approach, craftsmen and weavers were sensitized about the benefit of the scheme. 162 self-help groups [4] (SHGs) were formed covering around 2,000 artisans [5] practicing five different crafts. All the SHGs have bank accounts and are at different stages of grading for credit linkage. Majority of the beneficiaries are below poverty line. The bottom-up approach involved local people in every decision-making process.
2. **Design Intervention:** In 'Tangaliya', uniqueness of motif is the use of dots or *Dana*. The motifs range from a single dot to elaborate arrangements of dots, like 'mor ki jhaad' (peacock on the bush), 'khajuri' (date palm tree), aambo (mango tree), 'karodiya' (peacock with diamond shape motif), 'haveli' (bungalow with three peacocks) to name a few. Given its unique techniques and graphic quality, new designs and contemporary motif language with colours referred from fashion forecast were introduced to create interesting products.
3. **Product Line Extension:** Products other than traditional wrapper were manufactured to enlarge the market—winter garments (muffler, scurf), dress material (designer *shawl, kurta*), fashion accessories (bags, mobile pouch) etc. were added to the product portfolio.
4. **Imparting Skill Training:** Skill training was needed to address quality specification, design improvement, product

diversification and efficiency to increase production and create marketability. In addition to training, sub-cluster level centres called shared resources and technology support centre (SRTSC) have been established for organizing design dissemination and product development workshops.

5. **Common Facility Centre:** To meet the demand of dyeing at the local level which otherwise would have been done from far distant Ahmedabad, Rural Development Enterprise Centre (RDEC) started functioning at DRDA compound, Surendranagar to provide basic infrastructure support to the clusters. It also performs the job of distribution of orders to the right production channels, monitoring, supply of inputs and establishing market linkages.

   A raw material bank of silk yarn was started on pilot basis at cluster in March 2008 with ₹ 0.3 million [6] investment by CARE India. As on September 2009, 650 kg. silk yarn costing ₹ 1.4 million [7] was distributed to 250 artisans. The initiative has witnessed 99 percent repayment where silk yarn has been extended with credit period of 15 days to 3 months.

6. **Federating the SHGs:** Besides creating SHGs, artisans have also set up a district level federation named Surendranagar Vankar Samaj (SUVAS). The federation which has been promoted with 2,000 artisans from all five craft communities is efficiently managed by a governing body comprising of 16 members (12 males and 4 females) and 3 office bearers. The federation received active support from CARE India and SAATH Charitable Trust. Members pay an annual membership fee of ₹ 51 and meet on regular basis to discuss common interest and issues. As an integral part of SGSY project, federation was set up to revive traditional crafts and make them commercially viable with better bargaining power at the back end while providing collective marketing expertise at the front end.

7. **Providing Platform for Greater Visibility [8]:** Besides supporting the cluster to initiate tie-up process with the larger retail chains such as Fab India Retail Pvt. Ltd., Vanilla, Harita Kapur etc., NIFT has also taken initiative to showcase the products of the Surendranagar cluster at its design studio at NIFT, Gandhinagar, and its outlet at Connaught Place, New Delhi. Crafts are also marketed through exhibitions and fairs.

The above activities had a fruitful impact on livelihood of poor artisans. The community public partnership model was able to provide the much needed support to the art for time being and a possibility for sustainable growth in long-term. Observing that 'Tangaliya' has uniqueness in the technique of weaving beads like dots into the woollen fabric and had been traditionally followed only in select villages in Surendranagar district, the idea of registering the craft under geographical indication (GI) was mooted. While on one hand, registration under GI would protect this traditional knowledge from unauthorized use, on the other hand, it would boost marketability of the product by highlighting its uniqueness, which would lead to economic prosperity of producers. Equity considerations received higher importance than prevention of appropriation by unauthorized parties while exploring the possibility to register the craft with the GI Registry. It was intended to use GI essentially as a marketing tool to create a niche for this unique art by marking rich cultural traditions, highlighting brand identity as well as signalling the product quality. It was necessitated to arrange for fair compensation for the custodians of this traditional knowledge through commercial gain.

NIFT articulated the process of formation of 'Tangaliya Hastkala Association', an association of 226 artisans spread over five villages in Surendranagar district. As the initiative to register under GI was mooted at a later stage, by that time the artisans had developed confidence on the hand holding approach of NIFT under cluster development project. It was much easier to reach the target group with that novel idea. The cluster development project had started benefiting the poor artisans by garnering higher producers' share in consumer's rupee due to better price realization from collective marketing which otherwise would be in the domain of master weavers who used to control the trade from providing raw material to procurement of final goods. Artisans were also benefited from collective bargaining at the back end.

Further, deprivation and marginalized conditions faced by the poor weavers was the binding reagent in the hope of a better tomorrow. NIFT represented the case through a Chennai based attrney to the Geographical Indication (GI) Registry on 9th June, 2008. An application was made for registering 'Tangaliya Shawl' under textile and textile goods falling in class 24. Clothing includes *shawls, sarees*, stoles including handkerchiefs falling in class 25 and home furnishings, rugs and mats falling in class 27. Finally, registration as geographical indications came by September 16, 2009.

Immediately after the product got the GI registration, it received a good media coverage which drew the attention of public at large—otherwise it would have cost heavy to promote an unknown craft among the public through advertisement in magazines, online promotions, sponsored columns, write ups in travel magazine to attract domestic as well as foreign customers. Query was generated from University of Art and Design, Helsinki to promote 'Tangaliya' in high end European product market. Business enquiries were also received from few craft exporter houses for possible business tie ups.

Talks have also been initiated with Gujarat State Handloom and Handicrafts Development Corporation Ltd. to procure order for 'Tangaliya' which would be sold in the former's craft outlets named 'Gurvi Gurjari'. Indext-C, a body promoted by Gujarat government for development of cottage and village industries has come forward to explore the possibility for joint promotion of 'Tangaliya' by highlighting

GI in their *Craft Haats* which are presently operating in Ahmedabad and Kutch. Interest has been shown by an NGO which runs showrooms showcasing crafts from Gujarat at different tourist destinations in the state to promote 'Tangaliya' on its rich tradition and uniqueness.

True that the diligent endeavour of the NIFT, Gandhinagar, over the years has been able to create a successful public-community partnership, has made a modest beginning in upliftment of the condition of poor weavers and saved the art from the verge of extinction. The still lying challenges in production and operation system needs to addressed as follows.

1. **Production Capacity:** Production of 'Tangaliya' is still facing the challenge of capacity enhancement and scale increase. This being a complex and labour intensive process can only be produced at limited rate. Using new weavers in creation of this product is not easy because it takes years for a beginner to master the art. Also income of weavers needs to be increased to attract more people towards the profession.
2. **Product Quality:** Skill of weavers is very important to maintain quality production and to increase demand for the craft. However, expertise of weavers varies from one person to another. Increasing the skill-set of weavers and creating best quality weavers in large numbers is still a challenge for NIFT. There is a possibility of supplying the product to a leading retail chain; however without solving the above issue, it will not be possible to supply products to reputed retail chains.
3. **Product Design:** The students of NIFT have been designing motif for products which has resulted in inventing new products with fashionable design. However, more such efforts are required to create innovative product with unique features. Some of the ideas that could be implemented in future are bringing new products which are typical for different Indian festivals and seasons, using

colour forecasting techniques etc. Also, it is essential to bring product diversification to match the offerings in private retail chains.

4. **Infrastructure Requirement:** More units for dyeing at local level are required to overcome the trouble of getting the job done from Ahmedabad and also to save cost. Only a handful of dyeing facilities at local level are available for weavers. A proposal has been forwarded to the Government of Gujarat in this regard.

'Tangaliya Hastkala Association' was formed to apply for registration of 'Tangaliya' under GI because individuals cannot apply for the same. However, 'Tangaliya Hastkala Association' can play a major role in future. NIFT has extended their full support for support and survival of the dying art 'Tangaliya' and with their persistent efforts 'Tangaliya Shawl' has been registered under GI. However, they cannot support the weavers forever. A successful business model has to be developed which can sustain the test of time. NIFT is already in third phase of hand-holding stage and after they fully relinquish, business model should be able to take care of itself. Without 'Tangaliya Hastkala Association', the market would be completely disorganized; the individual artisans would not have any bargaining power or marketing capability. So 'Tangaliya Hastkala Association' which was formed as a policy requirement for the GI registration holds a key responsibility as the custodian of the knowledge and its conservators.

Concluding Remarks

Given the dispersed nature of the sector, each handloom cluster is unique by itself and is surrounded by specific problems as well as prospects. While product from some clusters have established market but they face the problem of poor wages due to market control by merchants; some clusters face both the problems of declining market share as well as poor producers' share in consumer's rupee.

In some cases, the primary problem may be revolving around the inefficient backward linkage. This calls for cluster specific intervention rather than a uniform top down approach. Considering the multi-faceted problems faced by Indian handloom sector, it would be too ambitious to expect that GI registration alone could lead to significant socio-economic improvements of the community. GI has the potential to drive benefit towards the custodian of the knowledge but needs effective management in supply chain, market linkage, quality assurance, design innovation and product diversification with proper infrastructural support.

Annexure I

Procedure for GI Registration in India

Step 1: *Filing of application:* Any association of persons, producers, organization or authority established by or under the law can apply in the interest of the producers. Application to be made in prescribed format along with a statement of case at the office of Geographical Indication Registry, Chennai.

Steps 2 and 3: *Preliminary scrutiny and examination*: Examination report would be issued after thorough vetting by the expert group.

Step 4: *Issuance of show cause notice*: Any objection by the expert group would be communicated to the applicant which the latter can reply to, within two months.

Step 5: *Publication in the Geographical Indications Journal*: All applications are published in the GI Journal within three moths of acceptance.

Step 6: *Opposition to registration:* After publication in the GI Journal, the application is open for opposition by any person for three months. Applicant/s should submit counter statement within two months of receipt of the notice regarding the opposition served by the registry.

Step 7: *Registration:* On successful settlement of the opposition, GI is registered and certificate is issued in case the application is accepted.

Step 8: *Appeal:* The registration is open for appeal by any person up to three months with the Intellectual Property Appellate Board (IPAB).

Step 9: *Renewal***:** As a registered GI is valid for 10 years, there lies a scope of renewal.

Source: GI Registry, Chennai, India.

End Notes

1. Website of Integrated Handloom Cluster Development Programme (scheme of Office of the Development Commissioner (Handlooms), Ministry of Textiles, Government of India, New Delhi); http://edi-handlooms.org [accessed 20th March 2010].
2. Ibid.
3. *Dana* is made while weaving, taking minimum of three wraps and wrapping of fine threads around it.
4. Website of SGSY Project (Community-based Organizations formed under the Project), National Institute of Fashion Technology, Gandhinagar.
5. http://www.nift.ac.in/gandhinagar/cluster1_cbo.html [Accessed March 2010].
6. Ibid.
7. Ibid.
8. Ibid.

References

Akerlof, G.A. (1970): The Market for Lemons: Qualitative Uncertainty and the Market Mechanism, *Quarterly Journal of Economics,* 84(3), pp. 488-500.

Babcock, B.A. and Clemens, R. (2004): Geographical Indications and Property Rights: Protecting Value-added Agricultural Products, Briefing Paper 04, MBP 7, Iowa State University, Midwest.

Baeumer, L. (1999): Protection of Geographical Indications under WIPO Treaties and Questions Concerning the Relationship between those Treaties and the TRIPS Agreement, Symposium on the *International Protection of Geographical Indications in the Worldwide Context,* WIPO, Geneva.

Bérard, L. and P. Marchenay (2008): From Localized Products to Geographical Indications.

Correa, C.M. (2002): Protection of Geographical Indications in Caricom Countries.

Das, K. (2006): International Protection of India's Geographical Indications with Special Reference to ''Darjeeling'' Tea, *The Journal of World Intellectual Property*, 9(5), pp. 459-495.

Escudero, S. (2001): International Protection of Geographical Indications and Developing Countries, South Centre, Working Paper 10.

Girardeau, J.M. (2000): The Use of Geographical Indications in a Collective Marketing Strategy: The Example of Cognac, *Symposium on the International Protection of Geographical Indication,* WIPO, Geneva.

Gopalakrishnan, N.S., Nair, P.S. and Babu, A.K. (2007): *Exploring the Relationship between Geographical Indications and Traditional Knowledge: An Analysis of the Legal Tools for the Protection of Geographical Indications in Asia,* Geneva: International Centre for Trade and Sustainable Development.

Gupta, A.K. (2003): Sharing Benefits with the Conservators of Diversity: Use of Agricultural Biodiversity: A Source Book, Los Banos, Laguna, Philippines: CIP-UPWARD, 3, pp. 608-613.

Gupta, A.K. (2008): *G2G–Grassroots to Global: The Knowledge Rights of Creative Communities*, Centre for the Study of Justice in Society and the Centre for Global Justice at the SU School of Law, Seattle University, USA and MIT, Globalization and Justice: Interdisciplinary Dialogues. 21-22 February 2008.

Gupta, A.K. (1980), *Communicating with Farmers-Cases in Agricultural Communication and Institutional Support Measures,* New Delhi, IIPA.

Gupta, A.K. (1994): Compensating Local Communities for Conserving Biodiversity: Shall We Save the Goose that Laid the Golden Eggs So Long, Working Paper No. 1206, Ahmedabad: Indian Institute of Management.

Hopperger, M. (2000): International Protection of Geographical Indications–The Present Situation and Prospects for Future Developments, *Symposium on the International Protection of Geographical Indication,* Geneva: WIPO.

Jena, P.R. and Grote, U. (2010): Changing Institutions to Protect Regional Heritage: A Case for Geographical Indications in the Indian Agrifood Sector, *Development Policy Review*, 28(2), pp. 217-236.

Josling, T. (2005): What's in a Name? The Economics, Law and Politics of Geographical Indications for Food and Beverages, *Conference at Institute for International Integration Studies*. Dublin: Trinity College.

Josling, T., Roberts, D. and Orden, D. (2004): *Food Regulation and Trade,* Washington DC: Institute for International Economics.

Mascus, K.E. (2000): *Intellectual Property Rights in the Global Economy,* Washington DC: Institute for International Economics.

Natarajan, V. (2008): Indian Perspective of GI Registration, *Regional Conference on IPR Protection through Geographical Indications,* Hyderabad, India, 3-4 June, 2008.

Organization for International Geographical Indications Network, 2005, *The Future of Geographical Indications,* available at, http://www.origin-gi.com/index.php[Accessed 28th April 2010].

Richards, P. (1985): *Indigenous Agricultural Revolution,* London: Hutchinson Press.

Suh, J. and MacPherson, A. (2007): The Impact of Geographical Indication on the Revitalization of a Regional Economy: A Case Study of 'Boseong' Green Tea, *Area*, 39(4), pp. 518-527.

Suratno, B. (2004): Protection of Geographical Indications, *IP Management Review,* 2, pp. 87-93.

Textiles Committee (2007), *Pochampally Ikat: A Comparative Market Analysis of Pre- and Post-Registration Periods under Geographical Indications Act*, Mumbai: Textiles Committee, Ministry of Textiles, Government of India.

World Intellectual Property Organization (2006): *Intellectual Property Handbook,* Geneva: WIPO.

7

GIs: A Case Study of Sambalpuri Sarees

Raju K.D. and Apoorva Sharma

Introduction

Geographical indication (GI) of goods is a category of an intellectual property that identifies natural, agricultural or manufactured good as originating from a particular place, where a given quality, reputation or other characteristics of the good becomes essentially attributable to its geographical origin. GIs are covered as a part of Intellectual Property Rights (IPRs) under Articles 1 (2) and 10 of the Paris Convention and also under Articles 22 to 24 of the Trade Related Aspects of Intellectual Property Rights (TRIPS) Agreement.

It was protected earlier in the name of 'indication of source,' [1] 'appellation of origin.' [2] 'The collective rights are included in the TRIPS negotiations of the Uruguay Round and appropriate provisions were included to protect the well-known geographical indications. [3]

India, as a member of the World Trade Organization (WTO), enacted the Geographical Indications of Goods (Registration and Protection) Act, 1999 which came into force from 15th September 2003.

Geographical indication (GI) of goods can be defined as an intellectual property that identifies natural, agricultural or manufactured good as originating from a particular place, where a given quality, reputation or other characteristics of the good becomes essentially attributable to its geographical origin. [4]

The main purpose of GI registration is: (i) to provide legal protection to the product by preventing unauthorized usage of the product by others; (ii) promotion of economic prosperity of the producer of the goods/idea; (iii) assigning a form of collective monopoly right to the producer either within or outside the relevant geographical area; and (iv) providing legal remedy to the registered proprietor against unauthorized users. GI registration gives a protection to the product from unethical producers selling their low quality and priced products in the market and exploiting the reputation of a GI.

The Indian textile items are extremely varied and have a close linkage with ancient culture and Indian tradition makes its products most suitable to be protected under the GI Act than under other any other forms of IP protection methods. Although various State governments have taken initiatives to protect the handlooms originating in their state but it is only confined to GI registration. Only in few cases (Pochhampalli Ikkat, Kancheepuram Saree and Chanderi Sarees etc.) has the state government looked beyond registration by taking initiatives to ensure and maintain quality. The absence of an effective post-GI mechanism such as branding and promotion is the most deterrent factor in reaping the commercial benefits out of GI registration. While domestic registration of GI is a relatively easy task, not much has been done in terms of enforcement both in domestic and export markets.

Evolution of Geographical Indication

Human beings have always liked to have quality and genuine products in their possession, from the kind of clothes they want to wear to type of food they want to eat—everyone wants premium products. The term 'geographical indication' is relatively new in origin and popularized with the TRIPS Agreement. But the concepts such as 'appellations of origin', 'indications of source', 'designations of origin' and 'protected geographical indications' used names of places and distinctive signs for a variety of products as indications of geographical origin since time immemorial like Champagne.

There is a huge demand for authentic and original products from Banarsi silk to Darjeeling tea. This desire of mankind had led to the popularity of those products that have distinct characteristics originating from a particular region. This rising demand has also paved the way for many similar looking products flooding the market. Initially, the products with uniqueness and originating from a place in India were protected: (i) under Consumer Protection Act, (ii) through passing off actions in courts, and (iii) through certification marks. [5]

However, such legal provisions were not suitable enough to protect our goods in the global market where numerous look-alike goods rode on the goodwill associated with these products. The unethical practice of selling fake products in the name of reputed products for getting huge margin prices are rampant in India. Cheap power loom saris are sold as 'ikat saris' in the market for a much lower price than the original saris. The original producers suffer a loss in market share and reputation of their product. The consumers also do not have much information on the quality and the original price of the products. Therefore, in an effort to safeguard the interest of the producers and consumers, the concept of "geographical indications" was conceptualized.

GI Registrations in India

As per the data available till March 2013, 193 goods have been registered under the Act out of which 128 belong to the handicraft category followed by agriculture (46), manufactured (15) and foodstuff (4). Amongst these, handicrafts (128) constitute 66 percent of the total GI filings and in handicrafts, the number of textile GIs constituted around 31 percent of total GIs. GIs that are included in both handicraft and textiles (e.g. embroidery) were also good in number.

The state-wise distribution of textile GIs shows that the southern part of India is very active in GI registration with Karnataka leading the list, recording 16 percent of the GIs registered followed by Tamil Nadu with 12 percent of the filings. [6]

Analysis of GI registration in the textile sector indicates that textile sector records 42 percent (35 percent of textile alone and 7 percent of goods that belong to textile and handicraft sector) of total GI registration. The Indian textiles industry is extremely varied, with the hand-spun and hand-woven sector at one end of the spectrum, and the capital intensive, sophisticated mill sector at the other. The decentralized power looms/hosiery and knitting sector forms the largest section of the textile sector. The close linkage of the industry to agriculture and the ancient culture, and traditions of the country, makes Indian textiles' sector unique in comparison with the textiles industry of other countries. Indian textiles contribute about 14 percent to the industrial production, 4 percent to the gross domestic product and 17 percent to the countries' export earnings. It provides direct employment to over 35 million people.

The textile sector is the second largest provider of employment after agriculture. The Indian textiles sector recorded a significant recovery in spite of the global financial crisis, inflationary trends and volatility in commodity prices which led to built up of strong demand-side pressures. Thus, the growth and all-round development of this industry has a direct bearing in the improvement of the economy of the nation. [7]

The globalisation has brought about enormous challenges to the trade and industry; and the worst sufferers are the producers of unique textile products who lose their markets due to large-scale infringement of the product. The promulgation of Geographical Indication (GI) Act, 1999 by Government of India has created an avenue for protection of these unique products of the country. The GI Act stipulates protection of the market of the producers and safeguards the interests of the consumers of these unique products through registration and taking infringement action against the infringers. It is believed that the IPR protection of unique textiles products of the country with a pre-determined market linkage strategy would help in brand building of the products, providing market linkages, generating more employment opportunities and enhancing the income of the stakeholders.

GI Registration Process

In order to be protected under the Act, a good must fulfil the following conditions. Firstly, it must be natural or agricultural or a manufactured good. [8] Secondly, the name of the good need not be a geographical name proper (e.g. Pochhampalli Ikkat) but may include traditional non-geographical names which has acquired a nexus with the geographical region (e.g. Khadi). Thirdly, the good must possess a certain quality, reputation or other characteristics e.g. Baluchari sarees are famous for their graphic pullav. Lastly, such quality, reputation or other characteristic should be essentially attributable to its geographic origin. To illustrate, Banarasi sarees are descriptive of sarees made in Banaras and denote to the public a textile of distinctive reputation. [9]

The registration can be initiated by any association of persons or organization or statutory authority by writing an application to the Registrar. The application must contain the following:

1. The association of persons or producers or any organization or authority should represent the interest of producers' of the concerned good and should file an affidavit as to how the applicant claims to represent their interest.
2. Application must be made in triplicate.
3. The application shall be signed by the applicant or his agent and must be accompanied by a statement of case.
4. Details of the special characteristics and how those standards are maintained.
5. Three certified copies of the map of the region to which the GI relates.

6. Details of the inspection structure, if any, to regulate the use of the GI in the territory to which it relates.
7. Give details of all the applicants together with their addresses. If there are a large number of producers, a collective reference of all the producers' of the good may be made in the application and the GI. [10]

After the acceptance of the application, same is advertised in the GI Journal and within three months of the publication of the application, any person can file a notice of opposition. The registrar shall serve a copy of the notice to the applicant and within two months, the applicant should send a copy of the counterstatement, failing which the application will be deemed to be abandoned. Where the counter-statement has been filed, the registrar shall serve a copy to the person giving the notice of opposition. Thereafter, both sides will lead their respective evidences by way of affidavit and supporting documents. A date for hearing of the case will be fixed thereafter. Where an application for a GI has been accepted, the Registrar shall register the geographical indication. If registered, the date of filing of the application shall be deemed to be the date of registration. The Registrar shall issue to the applicant a certificate with the seal of the Geographical Indications Registry. [11]

The certificate of registration is valid for ten years and can be renewed further for a period of ten years from the date of expiration of the original registration or from the last renewal of registration as the case may be. [12]

The office of Development Commissioner for Handlooms provides financial assistance up to ₹ 1.5 lakh per item for registering the handloom items under the GI Act. So far, financial assistance to register 35 items has been provided by this office to various States. The various state governments have sought the Technical Assistance Service on Intellectual Property (TASIP) from the Textiles Committee for GI registration of unique textile products of their states. As of today, three state governments have sponsored the GI registration of ten products. In order to protect these unique products, many governments have been spearheading a nationwide campaign in the country through facilitating GI registration of potential products and technical knowledge transfers. As a part of the endeavour, the Textiles Committee have also facilitated GI registration for products like Lucknow Chikan Craft, Banaras Saree and Brocades of Uttar Pradesh, Khandua Saree and Fabrics, Pipli Applique of Orissa, Bandhani Textiles and Surat Zari of Gujarat, Paithani Saree of Maharashtra, Bhagalpur Silk of Bihar, Guledgudda Fabrics of Karnataka etc. The state governments of Kerala and Uttar Pradesh have taken the support of Textiles Committee for GI registration of some of their unique products.

Further, in order to convert the IPR protection of the unique products to tangible benefits for the artisans and weavers of these products, the Textiles Committee has prepared an action plan for implementation. The Post-GI initiatives is first of its kind in the country and is expected to empower the stakeholders in terms of increase in income, employment, etc. once effectively implemented in the GI registered products. As a part of the initiatives, the Textiles Committee has also initiated post-GI initiatives by facilitating preparation of product catalogue and hosting dedicated B2B web portal for Banaras Sarees and Brocades of Uttar Pradesh and Pipli Applique of Orissa. Moreover, various studies to study the market potential of the GI products have also been conducted with the sole objective of organizing market linkage for the product in the post-GI registered period. [13]

Case Study: Sambbalpuri Sarees [14]

The Directorate of Textiles and Handloom, Government of Orissa on 11th January, 2012, filed a GI certification for Sambalpuri Bandha Saree and Fabrics along with the 'logo' in the GI registry with the help of Rajiv Gandhi School of Intellectual Property Law, IIT Kharagpur. [15] Sambalpuri saree is a traditionally woven Ikkat saree from Orissa. There are different types of Sambalpuri tie and dye sarees; cotton sarees, silk sarees, silk and cotton mixed (Bapta) and coarse cotton sarees. Sambalpuri 'saktapar' saree, is the oldest form of Sambalpuri tie and dye saree. It has double Ikkat (described later) chequer board pattern and brocaded border of 'rudraksha' bead compositions. In fact, Sambalpuri cotton sarees have a smooth finish and a distinctly original border and pallu. Many traditional motifs like fish, conch shell, birds, animals and other floral designs are woven in the fabric. The Imperial Gazette observes, "the flower bordered sarees of Sambalpur are called Phulia; and peculiar to the district are sarees known as 'Hansabali bordered' or striped with fantastic animal designs".

The traditional weaver's community "Bhulia" are the main propagators of this art. The cluster consists of professional weavers (non-traditional) from schedule caste and few from schedule tribe (Kuli tribe) accounting for 60 percent.

Initially, the weaving with tie and dye was confined to Kapta, Lungi and a napkin made of 12's/16's/20's cotton yarns which were dyed in vegetable colours. The main colours were yellow (from turmeric), maroon (from bark of Aal tree), blue form nile and black (from hirakasi and Chakda seeds). Fabrics of vegetable colours were sometimes not fast and range of colours was also limited, forcing the tie-dye production into limited colours and so also the design. However, in early times, the weavers experimented with twisted cotton mercerized yarn and synthetic colours. The looms started widening mainly to 52" width for normal sarees.

One of the pioneers that helped in development of this cluster was Late Padamshree Dr. Krutartha Acharya who along with his four associates started their business with the production on a limited number of looms. Later, he converted his business in to a co-operative society named Sambalpuri Bastralaya registered during the year 1954 under "Bihar and Orissa Co-operative Societies Act" and established in Bargarh town.

Sambalpuri Saree

Office of the Assistant Director of Textiles, Baragarh was established and started functioning from 1962 to look after the interest of the industry. Similarly, Orissa Weavers Co-Operative Spinning Mill at Tora, a village adjacent to Baragarh started it's functioning during 1971 and acted as a forward linkage to the industry by providing major raw material input i.e. yarn.

Marketing support from Bastralaya/Orissa State Handloom Weaver's Co-operative Society—functioning branch of Orissa State Handloom Development Corporation at Baragarh was established to look after the weavers working out of the co-operative fold. It made the availability of yarn at a reasonable price at the doorstep of the weavers.

However, the early 1990s saw the intervention of private entrepreneurs which comprised of a number of master weavers and traders.

On the other hand, gradual reduction of Government subsidies, declining support from apex WCS, closure of Handloom Development Corporation, closure of local spinning mill, abnormal increase in yarn prices, and mismanagement at the primary WCS level were the main reasons for reduction in the number of active co-operative societies.

Composition of Cluster

The cluster comprises of master weavers who not only weave but also employ other weavers by providing them with raw material and buyback of the finished sarees. Usually, the master weavers are in joint families and share the responsibilities involved in the production and sale cycle. The master weavers also give colour combinations, technical guidance and graph as per the design. Sometimes they also supply the required accessories. The master weavers of the area play the most vital role in employing the local weavers and 40 percent of the weavers in the cluster are weaving under the master weavers whereas 36 percent and 24 percent weavers belong to the co-operative and independent category respectively.

They sell their product to apex WCS, to showrooms established in different town/cities and to the wholeseller/retailers in metros like Kolkata, Mumbai, Delhi, Chennai and Bengaluru etc. There are around 9,000 weavers in the cluster out of which, the majority belong to Bhulia tribe and the rest are scheduled caste. Their craftsmanship is excellent and unique in weaving traditional cotton tie-dye designed products. There are 19 PWCS and 138 SHGs functioning in the cluster. The cluster produces tie-dye fabrics for which preparation of wrap/weft as per the design is highly essential. Normally, the weavers do this for their consumption.

Still there are some weavers who exclusively work to produce tie-dye and sell it to other weavers. Such separate groups of artisans are 206 in number in the cluster. The clusters have a good number of high skilled weavers who by virtue of their excellence have received honour from the Central/State Government. Some of them are working as weavers whereas others have turned them into master weavers. The cluster has sixteen number of national and ten number of state awardees. The traders purchase the fabrics and sell them to the shops established by them at Bargarh/other block head quarters/villages and supply to big cities and metros. There are number of such persons who contribute to the activities of the cluster and thus play an important role. There are 24 cloth shops in the cluster dealing with local handloom products.

Other Cluster Actors

Raw Material and Accessories Suppliers: The cluster has eight numbers of big suppliers of raw material who procure cotton, silk, dye stuffs and chemicals directly from the manufacturer and act as wholesellers/retailers for supplying it to master weavers/weavers/traders/institutions etc. Besides this, about 8 to 10 village level traders are engaged who usually take the raw material from the big traders at Bargarh and sell it in the weaver pockets.

Apart from these, there are lots of support institutes which support weaving activities in cluster. They are as follows.

Department of Textiles and Handlooms, Government of Orissa is the main support institution for the clusters and executes various activities through its divisional and zonal office at Baragarh headed by the Joint Director of Textiles and Assistant Director of Textiles respectively. It executes all developmental programmes extended by the State as well the Central Government, coordinates textile activities taken up by other institutions and looks after the administration of the WCS, whereas the divisional office functions in the supervisory capacity with same aims and objectives.

An apex co-operative organization (BOYANIKA) helps in marketing of fabrics of the primary WCS through procurement, exhibitions and expos, exploring new national and international markets, and providing other improved inputs. Technical training and skill up gradation to the weavers is provided by the Weavers Service Centre, Bhubaneswar under Integrated Handloom Training programme (IHTP). The National Handloom Development Corporation, a Central Government undertaking in the business of making yarn business in cluster helps in organizing/facilitating dyeing training at the field level as well as out of the State for the dye-manufacturing units.

The District Rural Development Agency is engaged in promoting developmental activities in the District. It is helping the cluster with infrastructure support, working capital subsidies for self-help groups and training to weavers' SHGs. During the last three years, it has provided one common facility centre each in three villages of the cluster. Funds under special SGSY programme from this Agency are available for cluster development activities.

Padmashree K.A. Centre for Co-operative Management, Bargarh, organizes training programme for the employees, board directors and weaver members of the PWCS as well as the staff members related to the Textile and Handloom Department on the principle of cooperation and financial management system of co-operatives and other administrative matters including legal procedures. It works basically for the development of co-operative movement in the district.

There are also many financial institutes associated with the cluster including nationalized banks in which State Bank of India plays a pivotal role. It extends loan facilities to master weavers and traders through term loans and cash credit loans with an interest rate of 10 to 12 percent for term loans and 10.75 to 11 percent on cash credit loans. The cash credit loans operate for one year whereas the term loans operate as per the project report.

However, the securitization and authentication of various factors by the bank do not encourage some business people to avail loans from this bank. The Sambalpur District Co-operative Central Bank extends cash credit loan facilities to PWCS of the cluster. But due to heavy outstanding of the WCS with the Bank, such operation have now been stopped. It has also lent cash credit loan to limited traders only. Bolangir Anchalika Gramya Bank has extended marginal finances to some individual weavers and self-help groups. Sambalpuri Bastralaya H.C.S. Ltd., Bargarh, is the largest PWCS in the state and has mostly concentrated in the western part of the state. It plays an important role in the socio-economic development of weavers of western Odisha and specifically of the cluster. It provides large scale employment to rural SCs, STs and other backward castes of the society, including women. Since its inception, it has been working as a production-cum-sale society by supplying raw materials, providing technical know-how as well as marketing support under a co-operative framework.

Value Chain Analysis

Value chain can be defined as a series of activities of an entity of a cluster that serves to deliver value in the form of goods and services to its final customer as users. Value addition is estimated by consumer's willingness to pay. The difference between total value i.e. price of the product and the total cost of performing (value creating) activities is the margin. Cotton sarees and dress materials are the main products in the cluster. [16] The products are artistic in nature and equipped with various designs, which plays a main role in the value addition of the fabric. The principal variants of the products are single Ikat sarees (uses tie and dye mainly on weft) and double Ikat sarees (both warp and weft constitutes Bandha). [17]

Conclusion

Sambalpuri sarees serve as a classic example where due to the intervention of the government and other private players, the cluster has received an economic boost. Due to the initiative taken by the Textile Ministry, Orissa and various Co-operatives like BOYANIKA, it has helped the weavers—both master weavers and independent weavers to increase their average income by 13 percent. However, in order to lure the younger generation into this craft, steps must be taken to ensure that the benefit reaches at the grass root level. There is also a need for reorganisation of the chain to one that is more buyer-driven, rather than producer-driven (Dolan and Humphrey, 2000). Buyer-driven chains are those in which end-buyers (typically retailers or supermarkets) establish particular standards and practices for their suppliers and products and organise the distribution channel accordingly to meet those specifications. High-end retailers such as Fab India could play an important role as a chain organisation by working directly with the weavers to supply their stores with high-quality, made-to-order products. Such products could be marketed and promoted under a Fair Trade type scheme and/or as part of each company's corporate social responsibility (CSR) policy that could both add value for buyers and producers alike (Nadvi, 2008). [18]

At the same time, NGOs, co-operative societies and other

civil society groups have an important role to play in this process. Trust relationships in the chain are quite low and will require some sort of "honest brokerage" to facilitate transactions and also smoothen over cultural sensitivities that could arise as chains are organised more efficiently. Particular efforts will be needed to determine roles for master weavers in any reorganised chain. Clearly, master weavers have an expertise role that can be enhanced, but breaking down centuries-old power dynamics will be a major challenge.

The case of Chanderi fabric suggests that cooperation between different chain actors can be achieved. An important caveat is the mechanism by which external actors engage with or coordinate the chain. [19] Successful GIs in Europe have been established through centuries of interactions, with institutions and social conventions governing the GI having evolved over a long period of time. A risk with external actors governing these chains is that the ownership of the GI is diluted or removed from the territory of the actors in the region itself.

Neilson (2007) [20] remarks that in the case of GI coffee in Indonesia, external actors (in this case roasting firms) have largely expropriated the GI and its quality construction to consumers, rather than it coming from farmers through collective action. Renard (2005) notes that success of Fair Trade products has often led to increased power among those managing the Fair Trade distribution channel, at the expense of the producers.

Similarly, Bowen and De Master (2011) [21] point out that the institutionalisation of culture, as conceived through GI schemes, can influence the protected cultures themselves in ways that dilute or alter the products being produced. This suggests that while external actors play an important role in re-configuring fragmented value chains, they can also re-distort chains in ways that may not meet their stated aims. Further research is needed to elaborate more on this issue.

Suggestions for Protecting Handlooms through GI Act

1. Creating awareness—various case studies on the textile sector indicate that there is lack of knowledge about the effects of GI amongst various stake holders. While there are master weavers who utilize the GI tag to their profit, the main weavers or the main community which developed this art form, is not aware about registration and is not even included in the producers list.
2. To increase the competition, an institutional mechanism should be devised for registration and promotion of the act for achieving desirable objectives.
3. Non-availability of historical evidence of the traditional products is a matter of concern. It poses problem for filing GI application; it is necessary to address the issue properly as most of the producers may not be able to document the historical evidence of the product. Further, any change or innovation done by the community must also be recorded.
4. Although various State Governments have taken initiatives to protect the handlooms originating in their state but it is only confined to GI registration. Only in few cases (Pochhampalli Ikkat, Chanderi Sarees etc.), has the state government looked beyond registration by taking initiatives to ensure and maintain quality. While domestic registration of GI is a relatively easy task, not much has been done in terms of enforcement both in domestic and international markets.
5. So far, only one Part B registration has been done, that too of Pochhampalli Ikkat, there is a need for more Part B registrations.
6. Since most of the stake holders are poor, a government initiated program for helping the weavers to register their product must be initiated. Similarly, certain NGOs must be established that would help in the registration process and share the financial burden.
7. The post-GI measures such as promotion, marketing and advertising must be encouraged. Product promotion with

brand building with special emphasis on domestic market should be prioritised.

8. Further, certain guidelines must be developed to ensure that the benefit reaches to the grass-root level. Various case studies indicate that the profit due to registration of GIs is being distributed amongst the traders and the condition of the weavers remains the same.
9. After a product is registered under GI Act, there is a need for identification of the infringer of this product but the procedure stipulated in the GI Act may not be suitable for the cause of stakeholders, which needs to be addressed.
10. The legal means for prosecuting the infringer of the GI products is not sufficient in India. Hence, a proper legal mechanism should be put in place for proper implementation of the GI Act.

End Notes

1. There are two multilateral agreements dealing with indication of source: the 'Paris Convention for the Protection of Industrial Property' (1883) and the 'Madrid Agreement' (1891). None of these treaties, however, contain a clear-cut definition of the term 'indication of source' (See WIPO Intellectual Property. Reading Material, Geneva, 1998).
2. The Lisbon Agreement for the Protection of Appellations of Origin and their International Registration' (1958) defines, "appellation of origin" as the geographical name of a country, region, or locality, which serves to designate a product originating therein, the quality and characteristics of which are due exclusively or essentially to the geographical environment, including natural and human factors (Article 2.1).
3. Geographical Indications of India: Socio-economic and Development Issues, http://www.aiacaonline.org/pdf/policy-briefs-geographical-indications-india-socio-economic-development-issues.pdf, accessed on 01.02.2012.
4. Section 2 (e), The Geographical Indications of Goods (Registration and Protection) Act, 1999.
5. Geographical Indication (GI) Initiatives, http://textilescommittee.nic.in/GI-INDIA.htm (January 24, 2012).

6. http://ipindia.nic.in/girindia/journal/Journal_44.pdf (January 21, 2011).
7. http://texmin.nic.in/annualrep/arep.htm (January 15, 2011).
8. Section 2(f), The Geographical Indications of Goods (Registration and Protection) Act, 1999.
9. Article 22.1 of TRIPS lays down these three conditions for GI registration.
10. www.ipindia.nic.in/girindia/GI_Rules.pdf (January 14, 2012).
11. Ibid.
12. Section 18, The Geographical Indications of Goods (Registration and Protection) Act, 1999.
13. Supra at 5.
14. Diagnostic study of Bargarh Handloom Cluster District Bargarh (Orissa), available at http://www.msmefoundation.org/DSR_temp/Diagnostic percent20Study percent20Report percent20of percent20Bargang percent20- percent20Handloom.pdf.
15. Dr. K.D. Raju prepared five GI applications for the Directorate of Textiles, Government of Orissa on textile items originating from Orissa.
16. David Mercereau Clémentine Vignault, 2008 Coffee Value Chain and Geographical Indications in India. http://www.ifpindia.org/ecrire/upload/eco_projects/mercier_vignault_2008.pdf.
17. Ibid.
18. Nadvi, K. (2008), Global Standards, Global Governance and the Organization of Global Value Chains, *Journal of Economic Geography* 8(3), 323-343.
19. Das, K. (2010), Prospects and Challenges of Geographical Indications in India, *The Journal of World Intellectual Property,* 13(2), 148-201.
20. Neilson, J. (2007), Institutions, the Governance of Quality, and On-farm Value Retention for Indonesian Specialty Coffee, *Singapore Journal of Tropical Geography,* 28, 188-204.
21. Bowen, S. and De Master, K. (2011), New Rural Livelihoods or Museums of Production? Quality Food Initiatives in Practice, *Journal of Rural Studies,* 27, 73-82.

8

GIs in India: A Case Study of Banaras Brocades and Sarees

Tapan Kumar Rout and Shakeel Ahamed

Introduction

Banaras, the oldest city of the northern India is known all over the world for its religious affinity and as an important production centre for unique hand woven textiles. The hand woven textiles of Banaras are famous for its intricate designs and beautiful motifs since times immemorial. The artisans of these unique products put forth their imagination in form of beautiful patterns and motifs to bring liveliness in their products, which is well appreciated by the consumers of the contemporary world.

The artisans of the centre produce traditional weaves like silk brocades, sarees and ladies dress materials. These products bear generational legacy as the technique of production has been transferred from generation to generation in the artisans' family. With the change in the preference patterns of the consumers, the weavers are also producing different diversified products like curtains, cushion covers, bed covers and other home furnishing products.

The centre is not only providing livelihood to thousands of artisan families involved in the process of production but also supporting equal number of support service providers like traders, raw material suppliers, dyers, designers, loom makers, etc. who support the artisans in the process of weaving this wonderful artistic work. The brocade weaving of the Banaras is cluster based and scattered over Banaras and adjacent districts.

Historical Overview of the Cluster

It is believed that the hand woven textile industry came into existence during the Vedic period and reached its zenith during the Moghul period. Since Rig-Vedic period, India has flourished as a major textile producing centre. Even the Hindu Gods used to wear some gold-coated clothes in that period. The clothes for God have been usually prepared by zari and silk yarns. It is always interpreted as the earliest equivalent of the present day zari work or brocades.

The *Jataka* tales and other early *Pali* texts has also mentioned about the weavers (*tantuvidyas*) and the techniques used by them for weaving different textiles. In most of the historical writings, Banaras has been prominently mentioned as an outstanding centre for textile manufacturing. The growth of the centre is closely attributed to its close proximity to the cotton growing region. Banaras and its adjacent areas were great cotton growing regions during the earlier period. It may be the reason for the growth of the textile industry in Banaras. Even the *Pali* literature has mentioned the city as a reputed centre of textile manufacture, famous for its *Kasikuttama* and *Kasiya*. The *Majjhimanikaya* refers to *Varaaseyyaka*, known for its fine texture. The *Kasika Suchivastra* was probably some kind of embroidery.

The Banaras weaving industry reached its peak during the Moghul period due to the patronage of Moghul Emperor *Akbar*. From the *Akbar* period onwards, an uninterrupted account of the zari work and brocades in Banaras are available in *Mughal* and *Rajasthani* paintings. It is significant to note that in the sixteenth century, the old designs abruptly came to an end and the contemporary paintings and wholesale-personalized motifs were introduced keeping the taste of the ruling classes in mind. This was the period when more emphasis was given for floral designs than the animal motifs of the earlier years. During the Moghul period, this important product also experienced the influx of Persian motifs due to the presence and influence of Persian masters in the court of Emperor *Akbar, Ghias Naqshaband* being the greatest Persian master among them to the royal atelier of *Akbar*.

During the post Moghul period, the hand woven textile industry also flourished uninterruptedly due to the popular preference of the domestic consumers. The first census of India has elaborately mentioned about artisans community, products and the area of production. The *Zari* and brocade weavers seem to have been considerable in number as the number of their houses was about 580 at that time. The product originated from the Banaras city and as of today it is the main production centre. However, with the increase in the demand for the product, more and more artisans participated in the process of production as it was a lucrative profession by that time. As such, the production base has expanded to adjacent areas. As of today, the main production centres are Varanasi, Azamgarh, Mirzapur, Bhadohi (Sant Ravidas Nagar), Chandoli, Chunar and Chakia.

So far, as the product variety of the centre is concerned, the artisans are very much acquainted with the production of silk brocades and sarees. Among the different varieties of sarees produced at the centres, some popular names are *Jangla*, *Tanchoi*, *Vaskat*, Cutwork, Tissue and *Butidar*, which are made up of silk warp and weft, on plain/satin ground base brocaded with extra weft patterns in different layouts introducing Buties, Bells, Creepers, Buttas in ground, border and anchal for getting glamorous appearance. The silk brocades produced in the centre are world famous. The designs are influenced by the socio-cultural ethos of Hindus and Muslims on one hand and the Buddhists on the other hand. With the change in time and consumer preferences, the weavers of the cluster are also undertaking changes in the design and pattern of the product along with product diversification. In order to cater to the needs of the overseas and domestic buyers, the artisans are also producing home furnishings, silk dhotis, stole, scarf, muffler, mats, dress material, wall hanging, made ups like curtains, cushion covers, table covers, napkins, runners, etc.

The growing demand of the overseas buyers for non-conventional products is also another reason for product diversification. Even though the share of these products is negligible to the total production of the centre, still it is a good indication for future development of product diversification and growth. The newly diversified products of the centre are stole, scarf, muflar, mat, dress material, furnishing material, wall hanging, made ups like curtain, cushion covers, table covers, napkins, runners etc. One of the important components of this production centre is the intricate and cumbersome production process. The wonderful pattern of the produce has mainly been attributed to the production process. The process, which starts with the procurement of raw materials like silk yarns and golden zari, ends with packaging of the products. In between, the processes like sizing, degumming, preparation of warps and wefts, dyeing and weaving are involved. The artisans generally take 8 to 15 days for weaving a saree depending upon the design and pattern.

Socio-economic structure of the centre: Varanasi is one of the largest and oldest hand woven textile centre of the country and provides livelihood to more than 1,70,000 weavers and other support service providers in the production centre. The cluster also houses around 86 thousand looms. Even if the production centres are scattered around 5 districts of Uttar Pradesh, the main production centre and most of the weaving activities are carried out in and around the Varanasi city. Apart from Varanasi, other districts wherein the handloom weaving has been practiced actively are Mau, Moradabad, Lucknow, Meerut etc. It is pertinent to mention that most of the weavers are covered under the co-operative fold even if some weavers have been pursuing activities in individual capacity.

There are about 635 weaver co-operative societies in the cluster, of which 473 are active. The total number of workforce engaged in the weaving activity is around 1,71,430; the males constitute about 84 percent (1,44,000) and the females about 16 percent (27,430). It is interesting to note that the co-operative societies are not so attractive for the manufacturer and about 1,30,289 (76 percent) prefer to operate outside the co-operative fold. But the situation in other parts of the state is totally different, as most of the weavers prefer to undertake activities under the co-operative fold. The total turnover of the cluster is about ₹ 6,600 crore. Most of the products cater to the domestic market. However, with the introduction of the product diversification, in the recent past, the export of the cluster is picking up and so also the exportability of the product. The product wise statistics of the cluster is discussed below.

Silk is the major fibre used in the cluster and around 57.78 percent of the looms are engaged in the products of silk fibre. Around 27.50 percent of the looms are engaged in the production of viscose blend fabrics/made ups and 5 percent each of the looms are producing cotton and woollen products.

As the name suggests, Banarasi Saree, is the major product of the cluster. Around 67.40 percent of the looms are engaged in the production of saree followed by brocades at 28.89 percent. The recent inclusion in the product profile of the cluster such as stoles, wall hangings, ladies dress material control 2.24 percent of the looms. Home furnishing items are produced in the remaining 1.48 percent of the looms in the cluster. The employment is also distributed in the same proportion as that of looms.

Due to traditional and cultural obligations of the people of India, Banaras Saree is a sought after product during the wedding seasons. This encourages the weavers of Banaras to produce more and more sarees as compared to other products. Further, in order to meet the ever increasing demand, the power looms began to mushroom in the cluster and due to technological advances, the power looms overtook the handlooms in production of the fabrics.

During 2010-11, the production turnover of the cluster was estimated at ₹ 6,607 crore. Of this, around 37 percent was contributed by handlooms and the rest was from power loom sector. The sarees contributed ₹ 4,402.57 crore of the total production of the cluster followed by brocades at ₹ 1886.82 crore. The product-wise production turnover of the cluster is given in Table 8.1. Besides this, products worth ₹ 2642.87 crore were sold in the name of Banaras in the domestic market. These were the infringed products produced elsewhere and sold in the name of Banaras. The total market size of the Banaras products was estimated at ₹ 9,250.05 during 2010-11.

Table 8.1: Production Turnover of the Cluster

(₹ crore)

Product	Handlooms	Powerlooms	Total
Saree	1650.98	2751.59	4402.57
Brocades	707.56	1179.25	1886.82
Furnishing	36.16	60.26	96.42
Diversified Products	49.98	83.30	133.28
Others	4.79	83.30	88.09
Total	2449.47	4157.71	6607.18

Source: Author's own calculations.

Infringed Banaras Brocades and Saree

The globalisation under the framework of WTO has brought about a sea change in the modus operandi of the international trade. With the phasing out of quota in textiles and substantial reduction of tariffs under the Doha Development (DDA) Round of NAMA negotiation, the export of textiles has increased substantially. The major producing countries like India have also increased their export to different destinations of the world. The post-liberalisation phase has also created more competitive environment in the domestic market due to opening up of the economy to the external players. The traditional hand woven textiles like Banaras Brocades and Saree have been fetching a premium price since times immemorial due to its unique quality and intricate design. The premium price associated with the products has not only helped more than 1.70 lakh weavers and support service providers to earn their livelihood but has also helped in establishing Varanasi as an important hand woven textile production centre of the world.

The globalisation threw an open challenge to these age old traditional products in terms of infringement. During 1990s, the higher premium price attracted the manufacturers of other production centres to copy the design and pattern of the products and sell it under the name of Banaras Brocades and Sarees. As these infringed products are weaved through machines, the price offered is far less than the original products. Due to the use of the name Banaras for marketing the product, this dishonest business practice has created severe damage to the original brocades and sarees. The infringement has threatened the livelihood of the original weavers and marketability of the product and on the other hand the consumers of the original products are deceived.

During the last 20 years, the maximum damage to the product has been done by the infringed ones, which have taken the niche market associated with the product. The presence of the infringed products has ultimately reduced the brand value and premium price associated with the product, threatening the income and livelihood of the thousands of the producers associated with the product. It, not only threatened the very existence of such a unique product of the country in the domestic market but has also taken away the export potential of the product, which has a very good export market in the Middle East countries and US besides Asian countries.

The market size of the Banaras Brocades and Sarees is estimated at about ₹ 10,113 crore out of which a major chunk of the market is being captured by the power looms and duplicate products. The share of the power looms is about ₹ 4,500 crore, whereas the market share of the infringed products is about ₹ 2,913 crore. On the other hand, the market share of the original hand woven Banaras Brocades and Saree is about ₹ 2,700 crore only. Hence, more than 2/3rd of the market is captured by the products which are not original hand woven products but marketed by the dishonest business practices to capture the premium price associated with the world famous textiles. However, most of the power loom products sold in the market in the name of Banaras Brocades and Saree are produced by the power loom industry of Varanasi and other adjacent districts. The power loom industry has developed along with the handloom industry in the similar places of production with the advent of the technological development in the country.

Table 8.2 Total Turnover of the Centre during 2011-12

(₹ crore)

Product	Hand looms	Power looms	Total	Infringed Products	Total
Saree	1819.8	3033.0	4852.9	1941.1	6794.0
Brocades	779.9	1299.8	2079.8	831.9	2911.7
Furnishing	39.8	66.4	106.2	42.5	148.8
Diversified Products	55.1	91.8	146.9	58.7	205.6
Others	5.2	91.8	97.1	38.8	135.9
Total	2700.0	4500.0	7200.0	2913.2	10113.2

Source: Author's own calculations.

On the other hand, the infringed products are basically

originating either from the other power loom production centres of the country or from countries like China, Bangladesh, etc. The practice of infringement may be classified into four distinct ways i.e.

1. Infringed products manufactured and sold in the domestic market, i.e. in India.
2. Infringed products manufactured within the country and exported to the international market.
3. Infringed products manufactured in other countries and imported into India for domestic market.
4. Infringed products manufactured and exported/sold in international market.

The Banaras Brocade and Saree are experiencing the infringement problem of all these categories. These business practices developed over a period of time appears to have come into existence during early 1980s to fetch the premium price associated with the original products. The contribution of the market share by these infringed products has no doubt threatened the very existence of the original products and also the livelihood of the thousands of the artisans of this product. One important contributor to the sharp decline of the original one is the complex design patterns and weaving of the product. The hand weaving and design drawing pattern is very complex in nature and time consuming and hence the cost of production is high whereas the infringed products are machine made and cost effective. Since the design and pattern of the machine made low priced infringed products resembles with high priced original products, it became difficult for the latter to compete with the former. Ultimately, the original products are losing the market and premium price to the duplicate products.

Effects of the Presence of Infringed Products

The demand of finished sarees has gone down in recent years. As a result, the wage rate has declined to about half of what they were earlier. The existing wage rate for skilled works like weaving and designs varies from ₹ 150 to ₹ 260 per day after rendering service for more than 12 hours per day, whereas for support services like sizing, dyeing, finishing and packing, the wage rate varied from ₹ 80 to ₹ 160 in the year 2010.

Due to low wage structure, the industry's production capacity has also declined so also brand value.

Ultimately, the weaving families are increasingly shifting to other occupations like rickshaw pulling, etc. which appears to be more lucrative than this age old traditional industry.

Further, the prevalence of the system of intermediary both in supply chain activities and procurement of raw materials create new challenges for the manufacturers.

Even in some cases, the poor weavers are exploited as the intermediaries/ agents offer very negligible price for purchasing their products.

On the other hand, the money lenders also charge exorbitant rate of interest for lending money to the poor weavers. Lack of credible financial structure to support their activities is also affecting the sector.

In such a scenario, successfully completion of the Trade Related Intellectual Property Rights (TRIPS) under World Trade Organization (WTO) with the inclusion of geographical indication (GI) as one of the intellectual property rights (IPRs) has brought about a new hope for the protection of these age old unique products.

TRIPS Agreement under WTO

The WTO agreement on TRIPS, signed in 1994, stipulated protection of intellectual property of the member countries.

Geographical indication (GI) is the newest addition to the families of IPR and "identifies a good as originating in the territory of a member or a region or locality in the territory, where a given quality, reputation or other characteristic of the good is essentially attributable to its geographical origin (Article 22.1)". Some geographical regions acquire a reputation for origin of product with some specific quality and uniqueness. It is the quality or reputation that distinguishes the product from similar products all over the world. When GI acquires such reputation, there may be attempts by others to utilise it for their known advantage. Such action by others harms both original producers and consumers of the products. The original producer looses a part of the market share of his product and the consumer gets counterfeit goods without original quality and uniqueness.

Article 22 to 24 of Part II, Section I stipulate the TRIPS agreement and defines the nature and scope of protection of the geographical indications. The agreement talks about absolute protection for wine and spirit under Article 23 and general level protection for other products under Article 22. Further, Article 22 has described that unless a GI is protected in the country of its origin, there is no obligation by the member countries to extend reciprocal protection.

Article 23 however stipulated some additional protection to the GI designated wines and spirits. The additional protection provided to wines and spirits imposes an obligation on member countries to legislate for the protection of wines and spirits even if there is no risk of misleading or unfair competition. The discriminatory approach accepted in the TRIPS council was supposed to be the result of a continuous effort by European countries for the unique blended wines and spirits originating from their countries. However, the countries have agreed for the establishment of a multilateral system of notification and legislation of GIs (Article 23.4).

Even though the member countries have accepted the TRIPS council mandate on absolute protection in letter and spirit, majority of the countries are also insisting for same level of protection for all products. The discussion over the extension of protection to products other than wines and spirits started in the year 2000, as a group of countries including Bangladesh, Bulgaria, Cuba, Cyprus, Pakistan, India and others opposed discriminatory nature and additional protection and demanded similar protection for other products. However, their argument was negated citing the clause of Article 24.1, which stipulates negotiations for enhanced protection for wines and spirits only. Whereas, the promoters of this thought are of the view that this article refers to the products other than wines and spirits.

Geographical Indications (GI) Act of India, 1999

Prior to TRIPS agreement, the products with uniqueness and originating from a place in India are protected through some existing laws: (i) under Consumer Protection Act, (ii) through passing off actions in courts, and (iii) through certification marks. Such legal provisions are not sufficient to protect the GIs of India in the changing world scenario as innumerable foreign companies and traders are free riding on the goodwill and reputation associated with such renowned geographical names of Indian products for years.

India being a signatory to WTO and TRIPS, requires protection of its different products originating in India with specific quality and geographical origin so that the dishonest business practices cannot replicate the products for their own advantage. If not protected in time, the producers of other countries can use the quality and uniqueness for exploiting the market for their own advantage. For example, the tea producers of Kenya can use the world famous appellation of "Darjeeling" on the package of their tea with the aim of free riding on the renown associated with it, and encroach upon the existing market of Darjeeling tea. Ultimately, the producer of the Darjeeling tea will be the loser. India could not prevent a Texas based company from selling rice produced in America as traditional Basmati type or American Basmati. It is because the Basmati rice was not protected under GI. These products if allowed to be produced by other countries will become generic over a period and loose their geographical identity.

In compilation of the TRIPS agreement, India enacted the Geographical Indications (Registration and Protection) Act 1999, implemented in the year 2003. Under this Act, the Central Government has established a "Geographical

Indications Registry" with an all India jurisdiction at Chennai, where the right holders can register their respective GIs. The GI Act is to be administered by the Controller General of Patents, Designs and Trademarks, who is the Registrar of Geographical Indications. It is interesting to note that though Article 23 of TRIPS provides a higher level of protection to GIs relating to wines and spirits only, the corresponding provisions in the Indian Act does not restrict themselves to wines and spirits alone.

Rather, it has been left to the discretion of the Central government to decide which goods or classes of goods should be granted such a higher level of protection. This discretion has deliberately been maintained by Indian lawmakers with the aim of ensuring the 'absolute' protection of Article 23 for the GIs associated with products of India's export interest. Once a product is registered under GI Act, the applicant or a group of applicants can be registered as proprietor of that product. As of March 2013 more than 193 products have been successfully registered under the said Act. It is pertinent to mention that the products like Pisco of Chile, Champagne and Cognac of France have also been registered in India under the GI Act.

Why GI for Banaras Sarees and Brocades?

In Banaras cluster, about 1,50,000 weavers are earning their livelihood by weaving Banaras Brocades and Sarees out of which more than 40 percent are female artisans, most of whom provide support services. While being concentrated in Varanasi City, the activity has spread to surrounding villages of adjacent districts. The incidence of contractor weavers and co-op societies selling directly to traders/others outside Banaras is very limited. The manufacturers in the cluster are unorganised and most of them are not even able to enjoy the opportunities created by co-operative movement by the government. The products, which are produced out of generational legacy has not only provided livelihood to the producers but also preserves one of the beautiful cultural heritage of the country produced so far. However, the economic condition of the stakeholders associated with the products is deteriorating day by day. The economic backwardness of the weavers is due to plethora of factors. In the weaving industry of Banaras, imitation is one of the major areas of concern.

The product with a unique design, pattern and texture commands a high price but once the design comes out from the manufacturing centre, the product is immediately copied by large manufacturers and power looms in the country. Further, the opening up of economy under the framework of globalisation has added new dimensions to the process of infringement as some of the manufacturers of other countries are replicating and selling their products in the name of Banaras Brocades and Saree both in domestic and international market. As soon as the design is copied, the product gets devalued. The original producers have to bear this loss. Since change of product invariably involves substantial investment, it affects the weavers adversely.

The effect is quite alarming. The exploitation in the sector has reached such serious proportions that many skilled artisans have been compelled to shift their age old profession of weaving to other works like making incense sticks, peeling and selling green *chanas* (seasonal work) and the women have begun to do domestic labour in the homes of middle class families in their neighbourhood. In addition, weavers are leaving Varanasi and migrating to Surat. In cities like Surat, many weavers are ironically joining the 'duplicate' Banarasi saree manufacturing process, as it is becoming increasingly economically viable to do that.

Influx of thousands of 'unskilled' workers into weaving from the rural hinterland due to exigencies in their areas coupled with the abandoning of the sector by rare skilled crafts persons, if left unchecked could sound death knell of the sector itself, thus depriving mankind of one of its finest traditions. Although the Handloom Reservation Act of India has reserved some products for the handloom sector, yet Act is silent about the protection of unique and original products of the country like Banaras Brocades and Sarees. In such a scenario, the protection under GI could save this famous artistic work of the country.

Article 22: Protection of the Product

The mandate of the TRIPS agreement has included GI as one of the IPR for the protection of unique hand woven products of the member countries. As per the mandate, the member countries can seek protection for the GI designated products in other member countries once it is registered in the domestic country. One of the interesting outcomes of the agreement is that until and unless the product is protected in the domestic country, the stakeholders of the product cannot claim/take action against the infringement of the product in other countries. Hence, it is very much essential to register the product in the own country to safeguard the product as per the mandate of the TRIPS agreement.

In India, the product has already been registered under the GI Act, 1999. The registration was effected by the Textiles Committee, a Government of India organisation in 2010 with the support of the producers' association and state government.

Article 23

One of the important controversial aspects of the product is the absolute protection to GI designated wines and spirits under Article 23 of the TRIPS agreement. Now the question arises that does the absolute protection for Banaras Brocades and Saree is necessary? To answer the question let us analyse the various components of Article 23.

1. Article 23.1 stipulates the members to provide the legal means for interested parties to prevent the use of a geographical indication for products, "...not originating in the place indicated by the geographical indication in question, even where the true origin of the goods is indicated...". In absence of such protection for the

product, it would be possible for the producers of the other countries say China to use the name Banaras Brocade and Sarees for products originating form China, if it is not protected in the same country.

2. Article 23.1 prohibits the use of geographical indication if "...the geographical indication is used in translation...". Lack of this protection of the product may pose a threat as the popular brand name may be used by the producers of other products, say food items, hosiery products etc. in case of lack of country specific registration and protection of the product.
3. Article 23.1 prohibits the use of geographical indication, "accompanied by expressions such as kind, type, style, imitation or the like". As this is not applicable for saree and brocades, it would be possible for example, for the producers of China to put the word words like imitation of Banaras Brocades and Saree on its silk products but they cannot use the logo if protected in the respective country say China or stopped at the border.
4. Article 23.2 stipulates, "that the registration of the trademark for wines which contains or consists of a geographical indication identifying wines or spirits which contains or consists of a geographical indication identifying spirits shall be refused or invalidated, ex-officio if a members legislation so permits or at the request of an interested party, with respect to such wines or spirits not having this origin". These aspects of the article may not be applicable for products like Banaras Brocades and Sarees.
5. Article 23.3 deals with homonymous geographical indications and provides that, "in the case of homonymous geographical indication for wines, protection shall be accorded to each indication". Homonymous geographical indication may not be a problem for almost all GIs coming out of India.
6. Article 23.3 talks that, "...the establishment of multilateral system of notification and registration of geographical

indication for wines eligible for protection in those members participating in the system". In the present circumstances, a legally enforceable multilateral system could be the only benefit for extension of Article 23 protection to other products like Banaras Brocades and Sarees.

One important element of the TRIPS agreement is that the member countries will have to decide on the mode of protection of geographical indications. As of now, different countries are using different modes of protection for the purpose. These are: (a) a sui generic law, (b) certification or collective marks under trademark laws, and (c) under unfair competition or consumer protection laws. In the countries which protect the GI designated products under sui generic law/certification or collective marks under trademark laws, a logo could be more appropriate to protect the GI designated products. In this case, the original producers can stop counterfeit goods only by proving that the infringed producers are not authorised to use logo, as they do not produce it in the region which the GI logo stipulates.

On the other hand, it is difficult to protect the GI designated products through logo in the countries, which applies unfair competition law or consumer protection law. In these countries, the infringement of the products can be stopped in the court of law with the proof that the consumers are misled because the consumers identify logo of the GI designated products for originality. In case of non-use of logo as a protection of registration, it may be difficult to prove that the consumers are deceived due to presence of counterfeit goods in the market. However, not many countries are protecting the GI through unfair competition or consumer protection laws. It may be an added advantage in the process of protection of GI designated products across the world.

In the above analysis, it appears that Article 23 helps the producers to prove the receipt by consumers of counterfeit goods in an easier way than under Article 22 of the agreement.

Conclusion

Hence, the arguments put forward for additional protection to all products under Article 23 appears to be valid and sound logical. Further, the absolute protection will also create a better avenue for products like Banaras Brocades and Sarees than the present level of protection. It would have been better, if there was no enhanced level of protection for wines and spirit and all the products are treated with equal importance. Since it has already been a part of the agreement, we have to live with it—but a pertinent question arises—are developing countries justified in demanding enhanced protection for other products? There is no doubt that the developing countries are justified in demanding higher level of protection, but in the present scenario, they should try to experiment the effectiveness of Article 22 for protecting the originality of the products and eliminating the infringement.

In the Indian context, the Act has eliminated such a discriminatory treatment at least for the domestic market. Hence, the registration of the product is a right step in right direction for protecting such unique products from infringement.

References

"Banarasi Brocades", (ed.) Ajit Mukherjee, Crafts Museum, New Delhi.

Dwijen Rangnekar, Senior Research Fellow, School of Public Policy, University College London, "Geographical Indications: A Review of Proposals at the TRIPS Council-Extending Article 23 to Products other than Wines and Spirits", Issue Paper No. 4, UNCTAD-ICTSD.

Elizabeth Barham, "Translating Terroir: The Global Challenge of French AOC Labelling" *Journal of Rural Studies,* 19 (2003).

International Trademark Association, (2002): "Doha's Impact on TRIPS: Balancing Geographical Indications (GIs) Protection", organised by the International Trademark Association (INTA).

K. Puri, "Is Traditional or Cultural Knowledge a Form of Intellectual Property?", Paper presented at the Oxford Intellectual Property Research Centre, 18th January 2000, http://www.oiprc.ox.ac.uk/EJWP0100.pdf, September 2002).

Policy Brief, No. 8, (2004): Geographical Indications under TRIPS Protection Regime and Development in Asia.

Substantive Obligations: 2.3 Geographical Indications, Prepared for the UNCTAD/ICTSD Capacity Building Project on Intellectual Property Rights and Sustainable Development, Geneva,. available at,
http://www.iprsonline.org/unctadictsd/ResourceBookIndex.htm.

Textiles Committee (2009), Dream of Weaving: Study and Documentation of Banaras Sarees and Brocades.

WIPO Secretariat, "Final Report on National Experiences with the Legal Protection of Expressions of Folklore", Intergovernmental Committee on Intellectual Property and Genetic Resources, Traditional Knowledge and Folklore, Geneva, June 13-21, 2002, WIPO/GRTKF/IC/3/10.

World Bank Global Economic Prospects and the Developing Countries 2002, World Bank, Washington DC, 2001.

9

Treatment of GIs under the Indian Competition Act, 2002

Bidyadhar Majhi

I. Background

In the literature of competition law, there are diverging views on the link between intellectual property rights (IPRs)/geographical indications (GIs) and competition law. One school of thought is of the view that intellectual property rights (IPRs)/geographical indications (GIs) and competition law are just like two poles that never meet. Accordingly, the scholars of this school of thought, better known as traditional school of thought, are of the view that granting IPRs to its holders or granting GI status to any product contradicts the very foundation of competition law. The prime objective of granting IPR/GI status to a product is to give the holder or the product the exclusive rights for his innovation or origin specialization, whereas competition law aims at creating a level playing field in the market for the competitors without treating someone or some product as special.

In a free market economy, ensuring competition in markets is essential to achieve the desired level of economic development. Of course, it is through optimization of consumers' as well as producers' surplus. Competition ensures optimum output and fair price of the products which in turn promotes consumer welfare and economic progress. On the contrary, an IPR is a privilege granted in recognition of the need of the holder to recoup costs incurred in the research and innovation process, so as to maintain incentives for further innovation and GI status granted to a product so as to recognize its specialty as originated in a particular place.

Thus, an IPR/GI entails an exclusive right for a limited time, enabling the holder or the product to charge a higher price than the marginal cost of production. As per the popular views, competition law can be applied to restrict the rights allowed to an intellectual property holder or GI status granted to a product as unlimited rights or special status, which may distort competition in the relevant market. This is the reason why many competition jurisdictions world over including the Competition Act of India, 2002 have not fully exempted IPRs and GIs from the purview of competition law.

In the above background, this paper is an attempt to highlight treatment of GIs under the Competition Act, 2002. It is to be noted that IPR is a broader concept which includes copyright and related rights, trade marks, geographical indications, industrial designs, patents, layout-designs of the integrated circuits, etc.

Besides the above introductory section, this paper consists of seven more sections including: (ii) rationale and sources of information; (iii) some conceptual issues relating to geographical indications; (iv) emergence of competition law in India; (v) important provisions of the Competition Act of India, 2002; (vi) treatment of IPRs/GIs under the Competition Act of India, 2002; (vii) linking geographical indications with competition law; and (viii) conclusion.

II. Rationale and Sources of Information

In the literature of competition law, many studies have been completed focusing on treatment of IPR under competition law and linking IPRs and competition law under different jurisdictions world over. But, with regards to treatment of GIs as a component of IPR, under the competition law over different jurisdiction world over, very little research work has been done. This paper tries to fill this gap in the literature of competition law. In this paper, an attempt has been made by the author to bring to the notice of the researchers/readers/stakeholders in the field, how the

Legislature in India has treated GIs while framing the Competition Act, 2002. That is, how the Competition Act, 2002 has reconciled the two contradictory objectives; one is to ensure level playing field among the players in the market and other is to give exclusive treatment to a particular player, granted by the government under certain other law. This research work is primarily based on the secondary information available on the literature of competition law and competition economics. Besides, information relating to IPR and competition law as available in public domain and research work done by other scholars in the field is also referred. However, due recognition has been given to the scholars whose work has been referred in this study in the reference appendix given at the end of the paper.

III. Some of the Conceptual Issues Relating to Geographical Indications

Geographical indications, a type of intellectual property, are forms of identification which identify a product as originating in a region or locality in a particular country. GIs are a place name used to identify products and is a sign used on goods that possess qualities, reputation or characteristics which are attributable to the place of origin. GIs may be used for any type of products including natural, agricultural and manufactured. Agricultural products typically have qualities that derive from their place of production and are influenced by specific local factors, such as climate and soil. Under World Trade Organization's (WTO's) TRIPS Agreement, protection of such products is mandatory for the member countries under Article 22. This provision has been incorporated in TRIPS Agreement keeping in view that geographical indications have to be protected in order to avoid misleading the public and to prevent unfair competition.

Though as per TRIPS agreement the member countries have to protect GI, such protection is not binding for all products. There are products in case of which geographical indications do not have to be protected or the protection of such products is given to a limited extent. Such cases may arise when a product name has become the common (or 'generic') term and when a term has already been registered as a trademark. Different countries formulate a wide variety of laws to protect geographical indications such as trademark law, consumer protection law and common law. Whether a product is recognized as a GI in a country depends on the law in this regard prevailing in that country.

There is difference between GI and trademark. Trademark is a sign used by a producer to distinguish his products from those of other producers, whereas GIs indicate that a product is produced in an area and exhibits certain characteristics that are due to that place of origin. GIs may be used by all producers who make their products in the place designated by a geographical indication and whose products share specified qualities. Unlike a trademark, the name used as a geographical indication will usually be determined by the name of the place of origination of that product.

IV. Emergence of Competition Law in India

The MRTP Act was the first economic legislation of India which came into force in 1969 and was enacted with a view to prevent concentration of economic power, control of monopolies, prohibition of monopolistic trade practices, and prohibition of restrictive trade practices. The substantive provisions of the MRTP Act, *inter alia*, sought to regulate concentration of economic power by making it obligatory for undertakings with assets worth of certain value as determined from time to time and dominant undertakings to seek the approval of the Central Government before effecting its expansion, adding a new unit or division of existing one or setting up a new unit of undertaking. With changing global economic scenario and initiation of economic reforms in India, the MRTP Act became obsolete and the need of a new competition law was felt. Accordingly, a high level committee on competition policy and law was established by the Government of India in October 1999 known as Raghavan Committee. On the basis of recommendations of the Raghavan Committee, the Competition Act was enacted in 2002 which was assented by the honourable President of India in 2003.

The crux of the enactment of competition law in a country is to facilitate economic development by creating a level playing field among competing industries/firms in a particular area of production by enhancing economic efficiency of the consumers as well as producers. Creation of level playing field in an area of production implies elimination of such practices which distort competition in markets in that area of production and which may cause or likely to cause an appreciable adverse effect on competition (AAEC) in markets. The essence of the competition law is to eliminate anti-competitive agreements including cartel, prohibition of abuse of dominant position of an enterprise and regulation of merger or amalgamation of enterprises which may cause or likely to cause an appreciable adverse effect on competition in markets. In many jurisdictions, horizontal anti-competitive agreements are presumed to have an appreciable adverse effect on competition. For judging whether an anti-competitive activity in the form of abuse of dominance of an enterprise or merger of enterprises will create an appreciable adverse effect on competition or not, the basic requirement is to identify the relevant market where such practices are taking place.

V. Important Provisions of Competition Act of India, 2002

The prime objective of the Competition Act, 2002 as enshrined in its preamble is to promote and sustain competition in markets, protect the interest of the consumers and ensure freedom of trade for the participants in the market. The rubric of the Act has essentially four compartments such as anti-competitive agreements, abuse of dominant position, combination regulations and competition advocacy. Section 3 of the Competition Act, 2002 prohibits anti-competitive agreements including agreements entered in relation to IPRs/GIs (beyond a reasonable extent). Agreement means arrangements or understandings between businesses which result in appreciable adverse effect on competition. Such agreements may be legal contracts in writing or may simply be verbal understandings made in an informal setting. Agreements not in line with provisions of Section 3 are deemed void. Section 3 also distinguishes between horizontal and vertical agreements.

Horizontal agreements are those agreements that exist between competitors of products which are substitute to each others from the consumer point of view. While determining whether products are substitutes to each other from the consumer point of view, factors such as end use of goods or service, physical characteristics, consumer preference, price of the goods and services are considered.

Vertical agreements are defined as agreements at different stages or levels of the production chain. Horizontal agreements are presumptively deemed to have an appreciable adverse effect on competition. Thus, agreements that provide for price fixing, big rigging or the sharing of a product or geographic market by competitors are presumptively deemed anti-competitive and void. In contrast, vertical agreements will be void only if it is demonstrated that such agreements cause or are likely to cause an appreciable adverse effect on competition. Thus, exclusive supply agreements, exclusive distribution agreements and resale price maintenance agreements will not be presumptively void. These agreements would be void if it can be demonstrated that they are likely to cause an appreciable adverse effect on competition.

Section 4 of the Competition Act, 2002 prohibits abuse of a dominant position. A dominant position has been defined as the position of strength enjoyed by an enterprise in the relevant market in India, which enables it to operate independently of competitive forces prevailing in the relevant market or to affect its competitors or consumers or the relevant market in its favour. Section 4(2) of the Act provides that there shall be an abuse of dominant position if an enterprise or a group of enterprises, directly or indirectly, impose unfair or discriminatory condition in purchase or sale of goods or service or impose unfair or discriminatory price in purchase or sale (including predatory price) of goods or service. For the purposes of this clause, the unfair or discriminatory condition in purchase or sale of goods or service and unfair or discriminatory price in purchase or sale of goods (including predatory price) or service shall not include such discriminatory condition or price which may be adopted to meet the competition or limits or restrict: (i) production of goods or provision of services; or (ii) technical or scientific development; or (iii) indulges in practice or practices resulting in denial of market access, in any manner; or (iv) makes conclusion of contracts subject to acceptance by other parties of supplementary obligations which, by their nature or according to commercial usage, have no connection with the subject of such contracts; or (v) uses its dominant position in one relevant market to enter into, or protect, other relevant market.

Section 5 and Section 6 of the Competition Act, 2002 deals with regulation of combinations. Combination in terms of the meaning given to them in the Act includes mergers, amalgamations, acquisitions and acquisitions of control, which are above a certain threshold. Broadly, combination includes acquisition of control, shares, voting rights or assets, acquisition of control by a person over an enterprise where such person has control over another enterprise engaged in competing businesses, and mergers and amalgamations between or amongst enterprises where these exceed the thresholds specified in the Act in terms of assets or turnover. If a combination causes or is likely to cause an appreciable adverse effect on competition within the relevant market in India, it is prohibited and can be scrutinized by CCI (Competition Commission of India), established under the provisions of Section 7 of the Act. As per the provisions of the Act, the acquisition of one or more enterprises by one or more persons or merger or amalgamation of enterprises shall be a combination of such enterprises and persons or enterprises, if certain specified conditions in the Act are satisfied. The Act has made the pre-notification of combinations voluntary for the parties concerned. If the parties to the combination chose not to notify the Commission then, CCI can initiate action even after post-combination, if that combination has an appreciable adverse effect on competition.

Section 49 of the Competition Act, 2002 prescribes for competition advocacy. Accordingly, CCI is empowered to take suitable measures for the promotion of competition advocacy, creating awareness and imparting training about competition issues. Competition advocacy activities are non-enforcement activities which are geared towards cultivating a competition culture and achieving competition neutrality throughout an economy mainly through its relationships with other governmental entities by increasing public awareness of the benefits of competition. The major tasks for the Commission under advocacy functions is to spread awareness about Competition Act and the CCI among various stakeholders, reach out to all the stakeholders including the consumers, the Government departments, industry organizations etc. through various seminars, workshops and symposiums to make them aware of the needs and benefits of competition, sensitize the stakeholders about nuances of competition law, to facilitate competition audit of their respective laws, and take confidence building measures among business enterprises and other stakeholders associated.

VI. Treatment of IPRs/GIs under Competition Act, 2002

As mentioned in the preceding section, Section 3 of the Competition Act, 2002 deals with anti-competitive agreements which have made an exception for IPRs/GIs. Sub-section 5 of Section 3 of the Competition Act, 2002 limits the right of the holder under: (i) The Copyright Act, 1957, (ii) The Patents Act, 1970, (iii) The Trade and Merchandise Marks Act, 1958 or the Trade Marks Act, 1999, (iv) The Geographical Indications of Goods (Registration and Protection) Act, 1999, (v) The Designs Act, 2000, and (vi) The Semi-conductor Integrated Circuits Layout-Design Act, 2000. It also preserves the rights of the GIs to prevent infringement and protect these rights, as long as the restrictions imposed by the enterprise dealing with GIs are reasonable, ensuring that competition policy does not interfere with the reasonable use of GIs. Implying, the Competition Act, 2002 has not fully exempted the enterprises who are dealing with the products which are granted GI status from the purview of the Act.

However, exemption has been granted to a reasonable extent of exercise of GI status to a product. The extent of reasonableness is to be assessed by the Commission itself without any prejudice. If the Commission believes that the concerned enterprise(s) has used the GI status unreasonably with a view to distort competition in the relevant market, it can initiate investigation against such enterprise(s) and impose penalty as per the provisions of the Act. The Commission is empowered to enquire into unreasonable conditions attached to GIs and can impose penalty upon each of GIs or enterprises which are parties to such agreements or abuse which shall not be more than ten percent of the average turnover for the last three preceding financial years. In case an enterprise is a company, its directors/officials who are found guilty are liable to be proceeded against and punished.

Moreover, under Section 27 of the Act, the Commission has the power to pass any or all of the following orders: (i) direct parties to discontinue and not to re-enter into such agreements; (ii) direct the enterprise concerned to modify the agreements; (iii) direct the enterprises concerned to abide by such other orders as the CCI may pass and comply with the directions, including payment of costs, if any; and (iv) pass such other order or issue such directions as it may deem fit. In case an enterprise dealing with GI products happens to be in a dominant position, is liable for scrutiny under the provisions of Section 4 of the Act, if it abuses its dominant position. However, the condition of reasonable use of GIs is equally applicable as is given for anti-competitive agreement. The GI product dealing enterprise does not necessarily create a dominant position per se.

Whether or not dominance results from the ownership of a GI product depend upon the extent to which there are substitutes for the product, process or work to which the GIs relates are available. The legitimate exercise of GIs by a dominant undertaking is not an abuse. It is, however, possible that the way in which a GI is exercised may give rise to concerns if it goes beyond reasonable. In case of abuse of dominant position by such enterprise(s), CCI can impose penalties like as in the case of violation of provisions of Section 3 of the Act and it has the power to order division of enterprise with a view to ensure healthy competition and foster ideal market conditions for the benefit of the consumers.

Further, for anti-competitive agreement and abuse of dominant position by an enterprise(s) dealing with a GI product, under Section 28 of the Competition Act, CCI may direct for: (i) transfer or vesting of property, rights, liabilities or obligations; (ii) adjustment of contracts either by discharge or reduction of any liability or obligation or otherwise; (iii) creation, allotment, surrender or cancellation of shares, stock or securities; (iv) formation or winding-up of an enterprise or the amendment of the Memorandum of Association (MoA) or Articles of Association (AoA) or any other instrument regulating the business of any enterprise; (v) extent to which, and the circumstances in which, provisions of the order affecting an enterprise may be altered by the enterprise and the registration thereof; (vi) any other matter which may be necessary to give effect to the division of the enterprise. CCI also may, during the pending of any inquiry into abuse of dominant position, order for restraining any party from carrying an act which is contrary to the provisions of the Act until the conclusion of the inquiry or till further orders.

VII. Linking Geographical Indications with Competition Law

The relationship between competition law and IPRs/GIs poses difficult challenges to the policy makers in the countries world over. In case of developing countries, such challenges are more pressing. The interaction between GIs and competition law is predominantly created by the non-rivalrous and non-excludable nature of GI products. The creation of this inherent tension is due to GIs being granted statutory rights which attempts to curtail such market power. Competition law does not encroach on IPRs/GIs holders and also, it does not question the exercise of excluding power as such against third parties, who seek to access GIs, but only the enactment of further anti-competitive behaviour aimed at exploiting the position of strength in the market in their dealings with third parties and the consequent generation of further anti-competitive effects.

It is only such further exercise, whereby the enterprise dealing with GIs product are used to leverage and expand market power beyond the essentially granted free riding function which can be restricted by competition law. Competition is not necessarily incompatible with GI and, on the contrary, can effectively lead to dynamic efficiency by protecting the originality of a product produced in a region/locality for the best interest of the consumer. There are concerns about this GI and competition law interface.

First, potential abuse of monopoly pricing, especially in developing countries, where effective substitutes to GI products are not readily available. Second, competition law seeks to draw a line between permissible business strategies and abuse of GIs, a line which is often blurred by horizontal agreements, exclusionary licensing restrictions, tie-in agreements, excessive exploitation of GIs and other selling practices. However, the limited monopolies granted by GIs are not *per se* anti-competitive; they only become anti-competitive when the GI holder looks to extend those rights beyond the scope granted to it. Competition law does not question the exercise of excluding power who seek to access the GI products, but only the enactment of further anti-competitive behaviour aimed at exploiting the position of strength on the market in their dealings with third parties and the consequent generation of further anti-competitive effects. It is only such further exercise whereby GIs are used to leverage and expand market power beyond the essentially granted anti-free riding function which can be restricted by competition law.

The protection is not meant to continue even after the objectives of GI have been achieved. In cases where GI is unable to prevent the extension of such power beyond the realm of the intended protection, competition is capable of playing this limiting role. Hence, the attitude of competition law to GI is not contradictory. It acts to ensure that the inherent purpose of the rights is not defeated, if and when the GI owner exceeds the essential function for which the status is granted. Such situation may arise when contractual exercise of GIs, results in competitive restraints, far in excess of the need to protect the owner against free-riding.

It may also happen when GIs grants such a degree of market dominance that compulsory license of the right to a third party is justified. In such a situation, GIs protection law may not be able to control the exercise of the right, when the consequence of such exercise exceeds the purpose for which it was granted. It is at this point that competition law becomes relevant, because it is equipped to deal with the consequences of the exercise of property rights.

Therefore, in such circumstances, the functioning of competition law protects the ultimate goal of GIs protection law, when the latter may be incapable of ensuring the same. A legal monopoly does not necessarily lead to an economic monopoly. The mere GIs do not lead to a dominant position in the market. By extension, the mere use of GIs does not constitute an abuse of the dominant position. The goal of competition law is not to prohibit monopoly; but to prohibit anti-competitive conduct. It accepts the achievement of an economic monopoly by means of research and development and consequent GIs as valid and legitimate conduct, which amounts to competition on merits. It recognizes the right to prevent copying even if it results in the denial of access to others. Pricing of GIs even by dominant firms is allowed to ensure adequate return on investments.

VIII. Conclusion

Despite contradictions between the competition law and granting IPRs or GIs, the ultimate objective of both is to protect consumer welfare, indirectly or directly. The Competition Act, 2002, like any other competition law world over, has made relaxation to the GI holders to a reasonable extent. However, the reasonableness use of GI status of the enterprise(s) is to be ascertained by Commission. The word reasonableness has been used with a view to strike a balance between the GI Act and the Competition Act. Moreover, unconditional exemption to GIs or in that matter to all IPR holders may distort competition in the relevant market which, in turn, harms the consumer's interest. Products originating in place having some unique quality need to be given recognition so that consumers are not to be cheated by the unethical business proprietors. Simultaneously, the enterprises dealing with GI product should not be given free hand to pursue anti-competitive activities which is against free and fair competition.

Thus, it has become imperative to strike a balance between the two. Sub-section 5 of Section 3 of the Competition Act, 2002 provides express exception to GIs, as long as they are exercised in a reasonable manner, within the boundaries of the rights granted under the GI Act. The competition law would need to deal with the manner of exercise of GIs only with reference to their effect on the market. The difference between policy decisions and individual case decisions needs to be maintained. It is not the existence of a dominant position that threatens competition in a market, but its abuse and competition law must be concerned only with the latter. When there is abuse of dominant position, it is irrelevant that GI status allowed the enterprise to attain such a position.

To conclude, it must be remembered that both, competition and GI protection law, as well as other IP laws should be applied in a compatible manner so that it would enhance consumer welfare without doing away with incentives to the individuals or enterprises who are engaged in the production of GI products .

References

Anderman, Steven (2007), *The Interface between Intellectual Property Rights and Competition Policy,* Cambridge University Press.

Bhagwati, J. (2001), Letter to Financial Times on TRIPS Agreement.

Burkhart Goebel (2003), *'Geographical Indications and Trademarks –The Road from Doha',* a paper submitted in the World Symposium on Geographical Indications organized by the WIPO and USPTO, San Francisco, California, US.

Chakravarthy, S., *Competition Policy and Intellectual Property Rights.*

CIPR (2002), *"Integrating Intellectual Property Rights and Development Policy",* Commission on Intellectual Property Rights, London.

Competition Act, 2002.

Correa, Carlos M., *Intellectual Property and Competition Law: Exploring some issues of relevance to Developing Countries,* Link-http://ictsd.net/downloads/2008/06/corea_oct07.pdf visited on 15.02.2012.

Geographical Indications of Goods (Registration and Protection) Act, 1999.

Journal of Competition Law and Economics, Vol. 6, No. 1, March 2010.

Kumar, Mohan (2003), *TRIPS: Geographical Indications,* Draft paper submitted to the UNDP Asia Trade Initiative.

Monopolies and Restrictive Trade Practices Act, 1969.

Panagariya, Arvind (1999), *"TRIPS and the WTO: An Uneasy Marriage.*

Planning Commission, Government of India, *Report of the Working Group on Competition Policy.*

T. Ramappa (2006), *Competition Law in India Polices-Issues and Development,* Oxford University Press, New Delhi.

The Agreement on the Trade Related Aspects of Intellectual Property Rights (TRIPS), 1994.

UNCTAD/ICTSD Capacity Building Project on Intellectual Property Rights and Sustainable Development, http://www.iprsonline.org/unctadictsd/docspolicypaper_sept 02. pdf visited on 14.02.2012.

Watal, J. (2001), *"Intellectual Property Rights in the WTO and Developing Countries",* Oxford University Press, Delhi.

10

Lesser-known Natural Goods as GIs in Indian Rural Economy

S.K. Soam

The Geographical Indications of Goods (Registration and Protection) Act ,1999 had been in operation since more than eight years, but the applications for natural goods are a few only. Therefore, the post-legislative responsibilities are even more important—these include identification of potential products, conducting socio-economic studies, initiating registration, and involving scientific and technical interventions for market success. The present paper identifies lesser-known goods as geographical indications (GI) in several states of the country, and also addresses some of the issues pertaining to use of GI as a tool for socio-economic development of the poor people in rural India.

Introduction

The main objective of the present paper is to share information about lesser-known natural goods in India, which can serve as a powerful tool in transforming the rural economy through registration as geographical indications (GIs). The knowledge about several products is so restricted that even the persons of other districts in the same state do not know about these products, while it has significant potential for domestic and/or international trade.

Therefore, creating awareness among the local key stakeholders and dispersing the knowledge about the product to the probable domestic and international consumers is another purpose of this paper. Third objective is to draw the attention of the corporate sector for association with the trade worthy products. Fourth objective is to draw attention towards scientific and technical necessity for establishing geographical link, uniqueness, quality up gradation and development of inspection measures. For the products of lesser-known nature, their registration as GI requires special efforts such as mobilizing people, arrangement of financial, technical and legal support. Therefore, the paper analyses the policy issues that can provide codal guidelines for utilizing the potential of these products for upliftment of rural economy through multiple protection as community intellectual property.

Andhra Pradesh

Agricultural Products as GI: Schedule IV Class 29: Fish and Meat Products: The fish and meat products are: [Maral/ fresh water fish grown in ponds and tanks known for special taste/Telangana region], [Dry fish and prawn/Visakhapatnam], [Pulsa fish/running water fish/East Godvari], [Judipee ram/goat breed with black spot and white hairs, unique taste of mutton/ Nellore district], [Judipee sheep/sheep breed for meat/Nellore].

Schedule IV Class 30: Rice Grains: Various kinds of rice available in the state are: [Warangal kitchdi or Ganpur khichdi/medium slender grain, good cooking quality/Warangal], [Sona masuri/Andhra], [Jelakara rice/Good quality rice/Nellore], [Medaki rice/Medak district], [Krishna katakala/red grains/Nalgonda], [Kurnool sona/fine rice/Kurnool district], [Chitti mythylu/scented rice variety of high quality/East and West Godavari, Warangal districts], [Molagolukulu rice/good organo-leptic character and sweetness/Nellore], [Itakaluloo/local variety/Anantpur], [Bandarkaluloo/local variety/Anantpur], [Godavari lsukalu/traditional variety fine grains with fragrance/Karimnagar], [Gidda mahsuri/local variety/East Godavari], [Nellore rice/high reputation/Nellore, Baptala, Kurnool].

Schedule IV Class 30: Spices and Condiments: Various kinds of spices available in the state are: [Mydukur pasupu/long type good quality turmeric, bright in color, high keeping quality/Kadapa], [Tekurpet turmeric/good quality turmeric/Kadapa], [Duggirala turmeric/local variety/Krishna and Guntur districts], [Armoor turmeric/local variety/Nizamabad], [Gokavaram chintapandu/less sour tamarind/East Godavari], [Rampachoda/tamarind grown in tribal region/East Godvari], [Charu mirchi/chilli variety bearing small fruits with high pungency/Srikakulum], [Warangal chapata/traditional chilli variety of deep color useful for pickle making/Warangal], [Guntur karam/pungent and dark red coloured chillies/Guntur], [Gollapalli mirchi/local variety of chilli/East Godavari], [Kohir zinger/red color zinger/Medak district], [Siddipet allam/zinger variety/Siddipet and Medak districts].

Name	Description	Place
Warangal or Ganpur kitchdi	Medium slender grain rice	Warangal
Sona masuri	Good cooking quality fine rice	Andhra region
Jelakara rice	Good quality rice	Nellor
Medaki rice	Popular local rice	Medak
Krishna katakala	Red grains	Nalgonda
Kurnool sona	Fine rice	Kurnool
Chitti mythylu	Scented rice variety of high quality	E&W Godavari, Warangal
Molagolukulu rice	Good taste and sweetness	Nellore
Itakaluloo & Bandarkaluloo	Local variety	Anantpur
Godavari lsukalu	Traditional fine grains, fragrance	Karimnagar
Gidda mahsuri	Local variety	East Godavari
Nellore rice	High reputation	Nellore, Baptala, Kurnool

Schedule IV Class 31: Fruits and Dry Fruits: Various kinds of fruits available in the state are: [Amrita chakarkelly/local banana/Khamam], [Balanagar sithaphal/ custard apple local variety/Mahboobnagar, Medak, Nalgonda, Warangal districts],

[Kohir jam/sweet and fleshy guava/Medak district], [Cherukurasam/juicy mango variety/Krishna district], [Chenna rasalloo/reputed mango variety/AP], [Pedda rasalloo/mango variety/AP], [Kallapur mango/local mango variety/Mahaboobnagar], [Swarnrekha mango/juicy mangoes/Srikakulum, Vizinagram and Vizag districts], [Nujiveedu mango/juicy and tasty mangoes/Krishna], [Allumpur benishan/quality mango/Mahaboobnagar], [Veerabalu benisan/quality mango/Kadapa], [Ulavapadu mango/mango with good keeping quality and taste/Prakasham], [Damalacherulu khader/good taste mangoes/Chittoor district], [Veerapalli mango/benisan mango variety with yellow red tinge and specific taste/Chittoor], [Chintalapudi punasa/local variety of mango/Krishna], [Banganpally (Benishan) mango/reputed and tasty variety/Banganpally village, Kurnool district but grown in large part of AP], [Palakollur battai/local sweet orange variety/West Godavari], [Pulivendla sweet oranges/high quality sweet oranges/Kadapa], [Pala sapota/very sweet and high fiber content sapota/Kurnool], [Vetapalem cashew/ local cashew nut/ Prakasham], [Palasa cashew/big size of cashew apple/ Srikakulam].

Schedule IV Class 31: Vegetables: Various kinds of vegetables available in the state are: [Krishnapuram Vulli or KP Onion/pungent, medium size onion known to have medicinal value and best for sambhar/Kadapa but known to be grown in Tamil Nadu also], [Guntur gongura/quality mesta used in pickle and sambhar/Guntur], [Madanapalli tomatoes/availability throughout the year/Chittoor], [Sareekanda/rhizomatous vegetable/Srikakulum], [Kakarakaya/bitter gourd of high bitterness found in black soil/Kurnool and Anantpur districts], [Jagatial long/local ridge gourd/Karimnagar], [Bara batlu/greens for curry preparation/Visakhapatnam], [Tanuku venkaya/green brinjal/West Godavari], [Indukurpeta brinjal/soft, smooth and tasty/Indukurpeta village of East Godavari], [Pounada venkaya/brinjal with specific taste like cheese/Srikakulam], [Baptala brinjal/round light purple color brinjal/Guntur], [Mula venkaya/local brinjal variety/Medak], [Bulli venkaya/local brinjal variety/Chittoor], [Poluru brinjal/spiny green fruits with white strips/Kurnool].

Schedule IV Class 31: Seeds and Grains: Miscellaneous kinds of grains available in the state are: [Sethama jonalu/good variety grain jowar/Chittoor and Kadapa districts], [Pecha jonalu/yellow jowar with good chapatti making quality/Medak and Khamam districts], [Maldandi/sorghum variety known for its specific qualities/Deccan plateau region], [Budama rice/drought and pest tolerant rice/East Godavari Agency area and Khamam districts], [Duda barulu/short duration rice/Kadapa], [Endudulu/dry-land rice/Medak], [Anupakaya/field bean/Jagatial and Karimnagar districts], [Madhire moong/long pods and good taste greengram /Madhure and surrounding areas of Khamam], [Chamki pesalu/green gram variety/Medak], [Sipai pesalu/greengram variety which is crawling type and resistant to drought/East Godavari], [Nalla pesalu/greengram variety which is resistant to cuscuta weeds/Srikakulam], [Nallakandi/black color red gram/Narayanpet and Mahaboobnagar districts], [Tandur Dal/red gram pulse with good cooking and long shelf life/Tandur, Rangaredddy district].

Schedule IV Class 31: Forestry and Horticultural Products: Various kinds of forestry and horticultural producs available in the state are: [Devarapalli vella mandu/locally available plant used for curing jaundice/coastal Andhra], [Jannaram teak/Adilabad], [Red sanders/high quality wood for making of artifacts and cosmetic products/Kadapa], [Red Aloevera/high cost medicinal plant/Anantpur], [Poraka/grass well known for soil binding properties/Mahabobnagar], [Chennur pan/quality betelvine leaves/Kadapa].

Schedule IV Class 31: Live Animals: The lesser known animal breeds in the state are: [Punganoor/white and dwarf cattle breed/Rayalseema region particulary Chittor district], [Chinlata devi sheep/sheep breed/Nellore], [Nellor goat/good breed for milk and meat/Nellore].

Schedule IV Class 30, 31 and 34: Miscellaneous Products:

The state also has miscellaneous products such as: [Arku coffee (schedule IV class 30)/quality coffee/Arku valley], [Kakimati jonalu (schedule IV class 31)/fodder sorghum/Chittoor], [Guntur tobacco (schedule IV class 34)/quality tobacco/Guntur].

Andhra Pradesh: Agricultural Allied Products as GI: Schedule IV Class 2 and 32: Traditional Knowledge Based Products: Several products have origin from traditional uses such as: [Gum kariya (natural resin under schedule IV class 2)/quality natural gum/Khamam], [Nannari sharbat (fruit drink under schedule IV class 32)/black color medicinal fruit drink made from roots of a creeper wild plant/Kadapa], [Jeeluga kallu/tree sap like toddy but not from toddy palm tree (non-alcoholic drink under schedule IV class 32)/Rampachedavaram agency areas of East Godavari].

Andhra Pradesh: Non-biological Natural Products as GI: The non-biological products are natural paints, ores and building material. The natural paints and ore are: [Colored clay (natural paint under schedule IV class 2)/clay used for coloring/Vizag], [Mangampet barites (natural ore under schedule IV class 6)/raw material for chemical and colors/Kadapa]. The building materials falling under schedule IV class 19 are: [Tandur bluestone/light weight granite/Tandur, Rangaredddy district], [Macherala madde/stones with greenish strips/Macherala, Guntur district], [Bethamcharla granite/quality marble for flooring/Bethamcharla, Kurnool district].

Karnataka

Agricultural Products as GI: Schedule IV Class 29: Fish and Meat Products: Lesser known fish and meat products in the state are: [Kane fish/popular brackish water fish/Udupi], [Bannur sheep/good meat due to special fat/Bannur in Mandya district], [Coorg pork/special non-vegetarian recipe/Coorg region]

Schedule IV Class 30: Coffee, Rice, Spices and Honey: Products in this category are, coffee: [Giri coffee/arabica coffee with typical aroma/Chikmagalur], [Chikmagalur coffee/high crown coffee/Chikmagalur], [Coorg coffee/reputed coffee/Coorg region], [Bababudangiri coffee/good quality coffee/Chikmagalur]; rice: [Bangar kaddi/local rice variety/Belgaum], [Gidda ragi paddy seed/dwarf flood resistant rice variety/Karnataka], [Gandasalae/scented rice small seeds/Dakshin kannada]; spices: [Byadgi chilli/dry chilli with extreme pungency/Haveri, Gadag and Dharwad], [Sankeshwar chilli/local chilli variety/Belgaum], [Ajjampura coriander/golden color excellent quality coriander/Chikmagalur], [Pedavagi chillies/specifc variety of chillies/Bijapur]; honey: [Coorg honey/reputed honey/Coorg region].

Schedule IV Class 31: Fruits and Vegetables: Lesser known fruits and vegetables are: [Nanjanagud rasabale/banana with unique taste/Nanjanagud, Mysore], [Munnavalli banana/local banana genotype/Belgaum], [Coorg orange/specific orange/Coorg region], [Matigulla brinjal/green round thorny brinjal variety/Coasal zone, Dakshin kannada and Udupi districts], [Perrigulla brinjal/round brinjal/Udupi], [Sakrepatha jackfruit/good taste, color/Chikmagalur].

Schedule IV Class 31: Live Animals: Lesser-known animals are: [Deoni cattle/specific breed of cattle known for high milk yield/Bidar, Gulbarga and Bijapur], [Melonad gidda/short statured cattle most suited to hilly regions/Uttara Kannada district], [Mudhol dog/highly robust hunter dog/Mudhol, Gulbarga district].

Schedule IV Class 31: Miscellaneous Products: Miscellaneous products include: [Bellary cotton/good quality commercial cotton/Bellary], [Maldandi/a sorghum variety known for its specific qualities/Deccan plateau region], [Gorankop greengram/local greengram genotype/Belgaum], [Red ragi/drought tolerant ragi variety/Kolar], [Mysore mallige/highly fragrant jasmine with bold and round flowers/Mysore], Udupi mallige/fragrant jasmine variety/Udupi]. The mysore mallige and udupi mallige also used for extracting the reputed essential oil, which is covered under class 3 of the schedule IV of GI Act.

Karnataka: Agriculture Allied and Non-biological Products as GI: Schedule IV Class 32: Traditional Knowledge

Based Products: Kokam fruit juice (Schedule IV class 32) is extracted from fruits of a local shrub botanically known as *Garcenia species* is a lesser-known but wonderful product. The fruit and juice has specific taste, and known as medicinal drink with properties of controlling diabetes, blood pressure and reducing weight. The juice is popular in Shimoga, Mangalore and Chikmagalur districts, and along Western Ghats coastal region. The major non-biological products are: [Kolar gold (schedule IV class 14)/good quality gold from kolar mines/Kolar], [Helakal granite (schedule IV class 19)/good quality stone/Bijapur].

Tamil Nadu

Agricultural Products as GI: Schedule IV Class 30 and 31: Miscellaneous Products: Among class 30 is one kind of tea [Nilgiri tea/good quality tea/Nilgiri ranges] and a spice [Erode turmeric/specific kind of turmeric/Erode]. Amongst class 31 there are horticultural products [Madurai malli/jasmine flower/Madurai district], [Salem mulgovo/specific mangoes/Salem and Dharmapuri districts], [Vayal vazhi/banana variety with thick skin/Trichy], [Virupakshi banana/good taste banana but susceptible to certain diseases/palani hills], [Kumbhkonam/Athur betelvine/betelvine famous in Tamilnadu like banarasi pan/Kumbhkonam] and a millet [Varagu/foxtail variety used in rice preparations/Yelagiri hills, Vellore district]. ponni rice

Schedule IV Class 31: Live Animals: The live animals identified in the state are: [Mechery sheep/specific breed for meat/Mechery (Salem district), Vellore, Dharmpuri, Namakkal], [Kilakaraisal goat/specific breed/Ramanathpuram], [Nilgiri sheep/specific breed/Nilgiri ranges], [Trichy black/specific sheep breed/Trichy], [Rajapalayam dog/a specific and famous breed of dog/Rajapalayam (Viruthunagar district), Mannarkudi (Dindigul district)], [Kangayam bullock/specific cattle breed for drought purpose/Kangayam taluks, Erode district], [Kanni Aadu/a tall breed of goat/Northern Tamilnadu], [Coimbatore sheep/a breed of sheep/Coimbatore], [Kombai dog/tall peculiar breed of dog/Kombai village near Kumbun town], [Toda Buffalo/semi wild buffaloes reared by toda tribe/Ooty], [Umblacherry cattle/specific breed of cattle/Tanjore], [Vembur sheep/tall breed with attaractive coat color/Vilathikulam taluka in Tuticorin district], [Madras red/specific breed of sheep for mutton purpose/Vellore, Chennai and around].

Kerala

Agricultural Products as GI: Schedule IV Class 30: Rice and Tea: This category includes several kinds of rice [Palakkadan matta/rice variety of red color bold grains with good palatability/Palaghat district], [Pokkali rice [1] /rice known for its environment friendly and organic method of production/Alappuzha, Thrissur and Ernakulum]. Rice for grains, and also for dietetic substances as classified under class 5 of the schedule IV: [Jeerakshala rice/scented rice organically grown by 'kurichiyas' tribe/Wayanad], [Gandhakshala rice/scented rice organically grown by 'kurichiyas' tribe/Wayanad], [Njvara rice/a medicinal rice/Wayanad] and a typical flavoured tea [Wayanadan tea/tea leaves/Wayanad].

Schedule IV Class 30: Spices and Condiments: Locally famous but lesser known spices are: [Telichery black pepper/dried black pepper/Telichery and Kannur districts], [Karuvilanchy/black pepper variety, bold seeds, high oil content, resistant to various stresses/Kollam], [Alleppey turmeric/high curcumin content/Wayanad district], [Wayanad turmeric/known due to specific characteristics/Wayanad], [Kuruppumpadi ginger/ginger variety highly fibrous and good diseases resistance/Ernakulum], [Alleppy ginger/known due to specific characteristics/Alleppy], [Alleppy green cardamom/quality cardamom/Alleppy].

Schedule IV Class 31: Fruits, Vegetables and Propagating Material: Fruits are: [Chavakkad orange dwarf/dwarf coconut cultivar with orange nut, good for nut water/Chavakkad of Trichur district] and vegetables are: [Chemparathi varikka/indigenous variety of jackfruit with red perianth/Kollam]. Propagating material of mango [Kurukkan/salt tolerant mango, polyembryonic with dwarfing effect/Kannur, Kasargod, Kozikode districts] and paddy [Koyama rice/stress tolerant, good straw content/Wayanad] [Cheradi rice/tall rice suitable for waterlogged conditions/Kottarakkara taluka, Kollam district] are important products in the state.

Schedule IV Class 31: Live Animals: The lesser known animal breeds in the state are: Goat [Malabari goat/a unique species confined to malabar/Malabar region], buffalo [High range dwarf buffalo/buffalo breed for meat/Wayanad], and cattle [Vechur cow/indigenous distinct line, very short stature cattle/Vechur, Kottayam district].

Madhya Pradesh

Agricultural Products as GI: MP is bestowed with number of GI products in agriculture. The unique, tasty and medicinal meat of Kadaknath poultry found in tribal areas of Jhabua qualify under class 29 as meat and eggs also. Kadkanath can also be a live animal (class 31); Soam (2005) has given the detailed account of this product as a potential GI. Important forestry product under class 31 are [Seoni teak/timber/southern MP] and [Khadkanag/a herb used to treat snakebite/Chikhaldara and whole Satpura ranges]. The other agricultural products are given in the following paragraphs.

Schedule IV Class 30: Rice, Spices and Condiments: The important rice varieties are: [Chinoor rice/scented rice/Balaghat], [Chatriya rice/scented rice, high fat percent/ Mandla]. Important spices are: [Kumbhraj dhania/coriander of good flavour and good oil content/Guna, Rajgarh], [Fenugreek/good quality fenugreek/Jaora, Ratlam, Neemach], [Amleta and Mahadev/good quality local garlic/Mandsaur, Neemach].

Schedule IV Class 31: Cereals and Pulses: The important cereals in the state are various varieties of wheat [Kathia wheat/durum wheat/Bundelkhand region], [Khurai genhu/good quality rainfed wheat/Sagar], [Sharbati/rainfed wheat bold seed, luster, good chapatti making quality/ MP and other states such as Punjab and Haryana], [Sehori genhu/good quality rainfed aestivum wheat/Sehore]; the flour from these varieties can be a separate product under class 30. The important pulses are: [Gadarwala dal/good quality redgram/Narsinghpur], [Kali moong/good quality local green gram/Sehore].

Schedule IV Class 31: Fruits and Vegetables: The important fruits are: [Chappara seetaphal/large sized custard apple with long shelf life/Seoni], [Kathiawadi mango/big size mango/Alirajpur in Jhabua district], [Sundaraja mango/sucking type mango/Reewa district]. The important vegetables are: [Malwa potato/low cholesterol potato with specific characteristics attributed to geoclimatic situation/Malwa region], [Baigani Arhar/white color bold seeded redgram/Mandla district], [Selana ki kakdi/good quality cucumber/Ratlam].

Jharkhand and Chattisgarh

Agricultural Products as GI: Jharkhand is famous for Lac, which is a scarlet resinous secretion of a insect thriving on specific trees produced at Ranchi, it is a natural resin, a product under class 2, the products such as skin cosmetics made from Lac would qualify under class 3. Under class 30, the important rice are [Gora rice/special kind of rice/all Jharkhand], [Kalimoonch/local rice variety/Jhabua region], [Chattisgarhi rice/local rice/ Chattisgarh known as 'Dhan ka katora' or rice bowl]. Under class 31, the important live animals are [Chota nagpuri sheep/special breed of sheep/Ranchi], [Chota nagpuri cattle/special breed of cattle/Ranchi], [Fighting cock/specific breed of poultry with fighting qualities/Hazaribagh].

Maharashtra

Agricultural Products as GI: The important products liable to classify under class 30 are: [Satara honey/honey known for taste and medicinal value/Satara, Mahabaleshwar], [Rethore basmati/scented rice variety/Karad region, Satara district], [Bhiwapuri chilli/local deep red color chilli with strong pungency/Nagpur], [Kolhapuri lavangi mirch/chilli variety/Kolhapur]. Among cereals that fall under class 31 are:

[Maldandi/a sorghum variety known for its specific qualities/Deccan plateau region], [Shalu jowar/a sorghum popular for high grains and fodder quality and taste/Solapur, Osmanabad, Bijapur(Karnataka)], [Jalki/jowar grain/Parbhani].

Schedule IV Class 31: Fruits: In this category, various fruits are identified specially several local varieities of banana, the fruits include [Bahadoli jamun/big size jamun fruit/Thane], [Bhagava anar/pomegranate of typical color/Malegaon], [Nasik grapes/small sweet grapes/Nasik, Pune, Sangali, Satara, Ahmednagar], [Katol sweet orange/sweet orange fruit/Vidarbha region], [Ahmednagar sweet orange/sweet orange fruit/Ahmednagar], [Hapus mango/mango variety/Konkan], [Keshar mango/mango variety of specific taste and aroma/Beed, Latur, Marathwada region], [Vasai banana/small size banana/Vasai in Thane district], [Basrai banana/dwarf banana/Jalgaon], [Jalgaon banana/banana fruit with typical taste and flavour/Jalgaon], [Sukeli/ripe big banana with specific taste/Vasai in Thane district], [Bhusawal kela/fruit banana/Bhusawal], [Ardhapuri banana/sweet, specific aroma, yellow color fruits of big size/Ardhapur in Nanded district].

Schedule IV Class 31: Live Animals: Various animals identified are cattle, buffalo and goat, the list include [Khillar/bullocks known for their strength/Sangali], [Berari goat/a local breed of goat/Nagpur], [Nagpuri buffalo/a local breed of buffalo/Nagpur, Yeotmal, Wardha], [Gaolao cow/a local breed of cattle/Yeotmal, Wardha, Nagpur], [Red kandhari/sturdy bulls/Nanded, Osmanabad, Latur], [Osmanabadi goat/fast growing, sturdy goat/Osmanabad], [Pandharpuri buffalo/buffalo breed known for high milk production/Pandharpur].

Gujarat

Agricultural Products as GI: Several agricultural products have been identified in the state. A local wheat and poultry are important products under class 31 and 29 respectively; these are [Bhaliya wheat/wheat grown in saline soil under rainfed conditions having special taste and chapatti making quality/Bhal region, Anand], [Ankleshwar poultry/specific poultry/Anand]. Among class 31, the live animals identified are: [Mehsani buffalo/sturdy buffalo cross of murrah and surati; dark black color/Mehsana], [Kankrej cattle/white dual purpose cattle/Ahmedabad, Gujarat; Nagaur, Rajasthan], [Surati buffalo/black small buffaloes/middle Gujarat], [Jaffarbadi buffalo/black heavy weight buffaloes/Jaffrabad], [Gir cattle/cattle known for high strength and high milk yield/Junagadh, Porbander], [Kutchi goat/dwarf, white goat for mutton/Kutch region].

Rajasthan

Agricultural Products as GI: Rajasthan is bestowed with several kinds of products e.g. 'mehandi of Sojat', which is henna for body painting grown and prepared at Saujat town in Pali district can qualify to be a GI under class 3. Several other products in the state relate to Section 30 of GI Act, 1999. The list include rice and various spice products such as: [Kali kamod/a local land race of paddy/Banswara], [Coriander of Kota/quality spice/Kota], [Bhichiwara ginger/desi ginger with specific aroma/Bhichiwara, Dungarpur], [Phalodi chillies/chillies of specific pungency/Phalodi region in Jodhpur], [Dungarpur zinger/reputed local zinger variety/Dungarpur], [Methania chilli/long chillies used to give color to dishes/Jalore, Jodhpur districts].

Schedule IV Class 31: Miscellaneous Products: Under this category, the products are cereals and pulses: [Malan makka/a local land race of maize/Udaipur], [Kanor urd/bold seeded blackgram/Udaipur], [Dungla urd/popular urd (black gram)/Udaipur], [Dohad yellow/a local land race of gram (Bengal gram)/Dohad, Sirohi district]. Flowers and fruits are also included: [Rose of Pushkar/rose flower for gulkand (it can be protected under class 29)/Pushkar], [Dhomas rose of Haldighati/rose flower for oil (it can be protected under class 3)/Udaipur], [Jhalawar orange/quality orange variety/Jhalawar], [Banswara mangoes/specific sour and sweet taste mango (*Aam* *papad* made of these mangoes is popular and can be protected under class 29)/Banswara and Dungarpur], [Chomu ber/ber fruit with fruit borer resistance/Chomu tehsil, Jaipur].

Schedule IV Class 31: Live Animals: The list include cattle and sheep: [Sirohi goat/A local goat breed/Sirohi district], [Pugal sheep/breed with white color body and brown face with strips/Pugal, Bikaner district], [Nali sheep/sheep breed having good carpet wool/in the region of Ghaghar river known as Nail], [Rathi/specific cattle breed of red color/Rath region of Bikaner and Ganganagar], [Tharparkar/well known cattle breed in desert of Thar region/Jaisalmer district], [Marwari sheep/sheep breed with black face and twisted ears/Marwar region of Jodhpur and Pali], [Marina sheep/sheep breed producing white wool/Avikanagar], [Barbari goat/very small sized goat prolific breeder/Jaisalmer district], [Beetal goat/specific breed of goat/found in parts of Rajasthan and Gurdaspur in Punjab].

Rajasthan: Non-biological Products as GI: The non-biological natural products include building material (class 19) and salt (class 30) as given ahead: [Kishangarh marble/pure white marble of repute/Kishangarh near Jaipur], [Makrana marble/Highly reputed marble for construction/Makrana near Jaipur], [Kota stone/stone as building material locally known as 'masuria'/Kota], [Samber salt/good quality salt/Samber lake, Jaipur].

West Bengal

Agricultural Products as GI: Schedule IV Class 29 and 31: Fish, Meat and Live Animals: Fish and meat are covered under class 29, while live animals are classified under class 31, the list of these products include: [Bairali fish/a typical riverine fish unique taste/Jalpaiguri, Coochbehar districts], [Bengal goat/mutton of castrated male goat has specific taste/WB], [Banpalal sheep/prolific breeder sheep with high quality meat/tribal doars in Jalpai guri, Siliguri and Darjeeling districts], [Ghunghru pig/prolific breeder pig with high quality pork/tribal doars in Jalpaiguri, Siliguri and Darjeeling districts], [Garole sheep/small size prolific breeder suitable to saline conditions/South and North 24 Pargana].

Schedule IV Class 30 and 31: Rice and Fruits: Rice and fruits are classified under class 30 and 31 respectively, the detailed list include: [Kalominia rice/black small scented rice/Jalpaiguri district], [Govind bhog rice/good rice/24 Pargana], [Baraipur guava/guava variety /Baraipur block], [Malda (Fazali) mango/well known mangoes /Malda], [Watermelon/watermelon with blackish cover/Sagar island], [Martamam/unique kind of banana/Hoogly and Nadia districts], [Darjeeling orange/a small size very sweet orange/Darjeeling].

Bihar

Agricultural Products as GI: The identified GIs are agricultural products in the class 30 (rice grains) and 31 (fruits and live animals), the extensive list include:[Kalanamak/rice variety/Eastern Bihar], [Chanpattia rice/small grain, scented non-sticky rice/Champaran region, Bettiah district], [Malda mango/variety of mango/Parts of Bihar], [Muzaffarpur litchi/famous litchi fruit/Muzaffarpur, Hazipur, Samastipur], [Makhana [2]/roasted seeds of plant found in ponds/Darbhanga], [Bachavar cattle/specific cattle breed/Muzaffarpur, Samastipur], [Gangatiri cattle/dual purpose cattle breed/Bhojpur district], [Shabadi/indigenous breed of dual purpose cattle and sheep/Bhojpur district].

Assam and Sikkim

Agricultural Products as GI: The identified GIs are agricultural products in the class 29 (fish, poultry), 30 (rice, tea) and 31 (fruits and live animals), the extensive list include [Indigenous ornamental fishes/ornamental fishes/Natural water bodies of Assam], [Puthi fish/fish variety of unique taste, fat content and shelf life/Brahmputra river], [Miri bird/local breed of poultry/Assam], [Chokoa chawal/semi-glutinous rice/Assam], [Komal chaul/glutinous and sticky scented rice with reddish grains, it can be eaten without cooking just by keeping in water for about half an hour/Middle and upper districts of Assam], [Aijung rice/rice variety/Kamrup, Darrang, Nalbari, Sonitpur, Barpeta], [Joha or Kolajoha chawal/ small scented variety of rice/Kamrup, Darrang, Lakhimpur,Dibrugarh, Sonitpur, Barpeta], [Bora chawal/glutinous rice with typical taste aroma and quality, used for making traditional cakes/Assam], [Assam tea/tea of high repute/Hilly regions of Assam], [Malbhog banana/banana variety/Kamrup, Darrang, Nalbari, Nowgong, Barpeta], [Sanchi pan/variety of betel leaf/Nogaon and Morigaon]. In the state of Sikkim, the important product identified is 'temi tea', found in the temi region of north Sikkim.

Uttar Pradesh

Agricultural Products as GI: Schedule IV Class 30 and 31: Cereals, Fruits and Horticultural Products: Important local rice varieties are: [Adam chini/aromatic rice variety/Varansi, Mirzapur, Chandauli districts], [Kalanamak/rice variety/Eastern UP, Bihar], [Swarn bhog rice/rice/Kanpur]. Cereals other than rice: [Bulandshahar local/maize variety with sweet taste/Bulandshahar], [Meerut local/maize variety with typical taste/Meerut], [Kathia wheat/durum wheat/Bundelkhand region], [Halna/variety of wheat/Farrukhabad district]. Fruits and vegetables: [Malihabadi Dasheri/dashehari mangoes of good quality/Lucknow region], [Gulawthi ke ber/a fruit known for its good quality/Gulawthi, Ghaziabad district], [Langda/mango variety/Eastern UP], [Chaunsa/mango variety/Eastern UP], [Allahabad safeda/guava variety of repute/Allahabad and adjacent areas], [Pratapgarh aonla/well known Indian gooseberry/Pratapgarh], [Jaunpuri muli/large sized long and tasty radish/Jaunpur]. Horticultural product: [Mahoba paan/betel leaf/Mahoba].

Schedule IV Class 31: Live Animals: The list includes cattle and buffalo: [Gangatiri cow/very hardy cattle breed/Balia, Varansi, Mirzapur, Gazipur districts], [Bhadawari buffalo/indeginous buffalo breed known for good milk/Agra, Mathura region, UP; found in MP also], [Tarai buffalo/indigenous buffalo/Pilibhit region].

Uttarakhand

Natural Products as GI: The agricultural products in class 30 include tea [Beninag tea/tea with specific taste/Almora]. In class 31, the important products are forestry product [Panchmukhi rudraksh/rudraksh used for holy purposes by Hindus/Dehradun, Haridwar], fruits and pulses [Harshil apples/famous apple fruit/Uttarkashi district], [Ramnagar litchi/popular litchi fruit/Nainital district], [Rajma/good quality pulse/Pithoragarh]. Under class 32 the identified products are agricultural allied products [Buraansh juice/juice made from red flowers of Buraansh tree (pink flower are known to be poisonous) Rhododendron/Hilly districts of Uttarakhand], and naturally available non-biological products [Natural mineral water [3] /pure water from Himalayas/Uttarakhand, HP and J&K].

Himachal Pradesh and J&K

Natural Products as GI: In HP, the listed products are tea [Kangra tea [4] (class 30)/ tea of repute/Kangra district and other areas of HP], fruit [Kinnauri apple (class 31)/dark red late harvested apple /Kinnaur] and vegetable [Pahari aloo (class 31)/potatoes produced in hilly regions during summer/all HP]. Agricultural allied product under class 29 is a sauce [Chamba chukh/a chilli based locally made chutney/Chamba district].

In Kashmir, the kashmiri kesar in general are quite famous but certain places add more value to quality of kesar [Kesar from phulwara/saffron with special flavour/Phulwara, and Kaishtwari kesar/a variety of vanilla (Kesar)/Kaishtwari tehsil of Doda district]. Other listed products from J&K are a special kind of pulse [Bhaderwahi rajmash/hill rajmash/Bhaderwahi tehsil of Doda district] and a milk product [Karari (class 29)/milk product sour in taste and used to preserve milk/Udhampur]. In Ladakh, a locally made fruit drink 'Tsetalulu' (class 32) from the berries of 'Sea buckthorn or Jadoo paudha' botanically known as *Hippophae rhamnoides* is very famous.

Punjab and Haryana

Natural Products as GI: Both Punjab and Haryana are famous for basmati rice, but there are certain specific basmati rice produced at restricted areas in the states and has specific and unique characteristics e.g. tarawadi basmati in Haryana [Tarawadi basmati/scented rice/Tarawadi, Karnal district] and sharbati basmati in Hoshiarpur and Gurdaspur districts in Punjab. The states are also known for various animal breeds [Murrah/buffalo breed known for high fat content and good quality milk/Rohtak and Hisar districts of Haryana], [Niliravi buffalo/Buffalo breed known for high fat content and good quality milk/Hissar and Karnal in Haryana, and Gurdaspur in Punjab] and [Beetal goat/Specific breed of goat/Gurdaspur, Punjab]. Among the category of non-biological natural product is 'Jamuna ka ret', the sand of river Yamuna from Haryana is very reputed in use of construction work.

Natural Goods as Registered GI

Specific Advantages: Several papers [5] are available citing number of benefits of registration of a product as a GI. In the Indian situation, following are the very specific advantages that can be accrued to the society through registration of natural goods as GIs.

1. Copying of the natural products is not possible but spurious products are sold in the market (seed, seedlings, primary or secondary products). GI registration would check and discourage it. GI registration would also check the adulteration of these products.
2. Specific characteristics provided by the nature would yield a premium on primary or secondary products. Marketing the specialty through corporate association can further shore up the sales revenue.
3. Uphold the reputation of the product, which is a rural brand earned in so many years. Popularizing the restricted rural brands among new areas and enhancing its consumption sphere.

4. Natural products are mostly related to farming and competitive products are very few. Therefore, registration of a GI must be seen as a tool for socio-economic upliftment of rural poor people.
5. Registration will inculcate and build up the entrepreneurship and marketing skills within the rural poor people.
6. Protection and conservation of biodiversity—because economic benefits accrued would encourage use of products from indigenous animal breeds and plant varieties and would also encourage adoption of environment friendly practices in so many products.
7. Commercialization of new primary and secondary products and to make them normally traded commodities e.g. natural mineral water from the Himalayas.
8. The registration would encourage formation of producers groups or commodity groups. These groups will be highly useful in so many things such as enhancing bargaining power in sale and purchase, organizing the highly disorganized agricultural sector, development of commodity specific database. These databases can then be used for responding to some of WTO agreements such as 'Agreement on Anti-dumping'.

Natural Goods as GIs: Specific Challenges and Policy Implications

Live Animals and GI: Live animals themselves as raw material [6] are certainly GIs [7] but geographical areas must be very specifically defined to avoid any conflict or dispute later as happened in the case of 'Melton Mowbray Pork Pies' [Dev Gangjee, 2006; Latha Nair, 2006]. Primary and secondary products received from animals or their products are also GIs; for example, reproductive or genetic material from Garole sheep or Feral goat. [8] Can animals by themselves be a GI because of the specific characteristics possessed by them as a result of gene-environment interactions occurring at a geographical location over a period of time? There is a strong case on the grounds that neither TRIPS nor GI Act, 1999 exclude them from registration

[9]; animals are normally traded as commodity, and therefore cannot be excluded if treated as goods. [10] Specific animals are found in a certain geographical region or ecological habitat such as wild animals or several animal breeds. However, all of them cannot be a GI. Thus, technical guidelines are required to draw a line between a land, race, breed and a GI.

Plant Genetic Resources (PGRs) and GI: PGRs include wild plants, local land races, farmers' varieties, extant varieties and released varieties. First, all the PGRs are not GIs, secondly any decision on GI registration or use of registered GI must be taken in consultation with other prevailing laws [11] in India. Certain wild plants have several medicinal uses but all will not qualify for a GI. [12] KP onion [13] of AP and Tamilnadu, Kanor urd of Rajasthan, Komal chaul of Assam and Pokkali rice [14] of Kerala are the perfect examples of a potential GI of local land races. In some cases, the influence of geographical region is very high in contribution of specific characteristics, therefore the type of variety does not matter much—the examples are Malwa potato, Sehori wheat, Khurai wheat in MP and Bhaliya wheat in Gujarat; such products originating from specific regions have specific morphological and nutritional characteristics and have been protected as GI in other countries. [15] Not all, but several of the farmers' varieties [16] would qualify to be a GI, the secondary products from such varieties must also be registered as GI. Among biodiversity and farmers' varieties, the establishment of product specific characteristics and geographical alienation would be a great challenge. [17] Some of the released varieties have taken a status of a GI on account of their longer association with a particular place and attainment of reputation. [18]

Marketing, Trade and GI: For profit maximization of trading and producer communities, the efforts should be done to encourage trading of secondary products [20], and marketing the specialty either directly [19] or through corporate association. [21] Scientific and technical interventions are required to ensure product traceability [22] in supply chain, product characteristics traceability through technological means [23] and product characteristics improvement through biotechnological application—scientific institutions and marketing establishments can together find new market segments for several of unknown products. [24] Protection and enforcement of community intellectual property rights such as community trademark is essential to establish a rural brand. The current efforts of Tea Board of India in case of Darjeeling tea [25] and Assam tea [26] need a special mention about the role of a public organization in defending the producers' interests.

Conclusion

Antiquity can certainly not be an essential requirement in natural goods especially agricultural products; some products have been evolved in so many years and are famous since ages e.g. traditional knowledge based products and local land races, but there are certain products, which have attained reputation quickly though took some time for geographical association e.g. released varieties. The main purpose of GI registry is commercial exploitation for economic upliftment of producers' community. In achieving this goal, the other socio-economic, ecological and environmental aspects must not be overlooked. Some of these aspects are conservation of fragile species and fragile habitat and environment, protection of depleting natural non-biological GI goods and protection of rural resource poor producers.

Government may take appropriate measures, lest in the wake of economic exploitation, the original producers are replaced by the large corporate sector. The rural poor may also face in-house competition with big players in the same geographical region in the form of large-scale specialty production, corporate farming or contract farming. The scientific and technical institutions have challenges for not only improving the GI goods but also developing scientific inspection mechanism. Scientific deliveries as a means of protecting and promoting community intellectual property rights are other bigger challenges for scientific institutions that can support other institutions, who take proactive action and lead in GI matters.

End Notes

1. Soam (2005) has given the detailed account of growing practices in symbiotic relationship.
2. Soam (2005) has given the detailed account of makhana grown in Bihar.
3. Swarnim Waglé (2004) in his policy brief, which is a part of the three-year Regional Programme on 'Securing Farmers' Rights to Livelihood in the Hindu-Kush Himalaya Region' of Hanoi based UNDP organization discusses the natural mineral water as potential GI with lot of prospects on the basis of futuristic demand of bottled water. He specifically mentions that "Natural" mineral waters, however, have to come from approved underground sources. Considered biologically pure, these waters are required to undergo no treatment other than physical filtration and iron removal. For further details please see www.sawtee.org. Soam (2005) discusses the potential of 'Ganga' water as potential GI.
4. Though its good quality tea, and also registered as GI but still a less known GI, probably due to more popular tea such as Darjeeling tea and Assam tea are available in the market.
5. Dwijen Rangnekar (2003) and Swarnim Waglé (2007) give the detailed account of GIs as socio-economic tool and its implications for human development respectively.
6. Pursuant to Article 2(5) of Regulation (EEC) No 2081/92 live animals are included as raw material under the provisions of Article 5 of Commission Regulation (EC) No. 1898/2006 dated 14th December 2006; the details are available in Official Journal of the European Union (23.12.2006, L369/1).
7. Author had discussed in detail the examples of various kinds of meats obtained from Black Bengal goat in West Bengal, Chegu goat in Himachal Pradesh and Kadaknath chicken in MP [Soam, 2005]. But for GI registration, the study of meat products such as 'Cordero de Navarra' or 'Nafarroako Arkumea' a registered PGI in European Union can throw light of procedural guidelines and requirements. This is a lamb meat, which is distinct in characteristics of live animal used for meat i.e. suckled by the ewe up to the time of slaughter (lechal) or up to 45 days from birth (ternasco), weigth of animal at the time of slaughter, and meat's distinguishing features. For details please see Official Journal of the European Union (2006/C 158/03), page C158/6.

In Indian situation, for Bengal goat, chegu goat and kadaknath chicken, there are few specific constraints: (a) Due to open breeding, the animals have become non-descript, its difficult to find original breed animal, (b) The inbreeding depression among herd is very high, and (c) The species are highly endemic and survival of species is already under threat, the GI registration may boost up the product demand and therefore make them further vulnerable if supplementary actions are not taken. Post-GI registration challenges for these products are scientific interventions for making enough population of descriptor animals and professional production process on the basis of established marketing principals i.e. originality and regular supply.

8. Garole sheep found in WB is a prolific breeder and can thrive on salt water. Feral goat found in Barren Island in Andaman and Nicobar exclusively thrives on seawater, and resists drought also.
9. TRIPS Article 27.3 (b) clearly mentions about exclusion of certain category from patent, but for GI such kind of exclusions have not been made.
10. The Surat Thani Oyster, a live animal has been registered as GI in Thailand (Reg. No. Sor Chor 49100010) on 23rd June 2006. Physical characteristics of the oyster have been given as the main basis of geographical link.
11. Mainly Protection of Plant Varieties and Farmers Rights Act, 2001 and the Biological Diversity Act, 2002.
12. Khadkanag, a herb found in Chikhaldara, Satpura ranges, MP is locally used to treat snakebite; Devarapalli vella mandu, a plant found in East Godavari, AP is locally used to treat jaundice. Establishing geographical link would be very difficult because the same plant found in other regions of the country or in another country would mostly have the same medicinal properties. Similarly safed musali (*chlorophytum arundinaceum*) grown in AP and Assam can be registered if these two products are different from one another; ashwagandha (*Adhatoda vassica*) can be strong GI if proved that it is different than the same product from China or any other producing country.
13. KP onion due to it typical pungency is reputed for use in specific south Indian recipe such as 'sambhar'. Latest research reports that Quantitative Trait Loci (QTL) controls pungency; there is a

significant associations of both pungency and bulb soluble solids content, and genetic markers may provide a practical means to select for lower pungency without correlated selection for lowered solids [John McCallum et al., 2007].

14. Author had discussed in detail the case of pokkali rice, the specialty is organic production involving high amount of community intelligence in rearing prawn together with rice in symbiotic system [Soam, 2005].
15. The Alcachofa de Tudela i.e. Artichoke, a registered Protected Geographical Indication (PGI) from 'Navarra', which is a wine region of north Spain. The specific charactersitics are morphological feaures, nutritional values of various minerals and vitamins available, and also the method of production. Details are available on 'www.navarra.com/gastronomia/alcachofas.htm' accessed on 23rd February, 2007.
16. A statutory authority constituted under Protection of Plant Varieties and Farmers Rights Act, 2001 is responsible for registration of farmers varieties.
17. For example, producers of sharbati basmati in Punjab, Rethore basmati in Maharashtra would be willing to differentiate their product from Basmati from Haryana Western UP or Uttrakhand. Similarly there can be cases of similar product in the same district with little differentiation, for example, Mydukur pasupu or turmeric and Tekurpet turmeric both are found in Kadapa district of AP but one has to check whether both are same or different.
18. For example, Bapatla rice or BPT- Rice, a variety developed at Agricultural University station, Bapatla, (AP) through selection from three way cross of Mahasuri (Japanese variety), GEB 24 and TN1. It was developed during 70s but became popular during 80s, and now also it's popular rice. Similarly, Warangal kitchdi or Ganpur khichdi a well known rice from Warangal, AP is a released variety HR 35 or GEB 24; RS Pura basmati (Basmati-370) in Jammu, Lok-1 wheat in MP are also a released varieties that can also be a GI. But in such cases, GI registry should ensure that proprietors of GI must be only those institutions, which bred these varieties, others can be authorized users.
19. Some of the secondary products are sehore wheat flour, seeds of

sehori wheat, mango pulp and nursery plants of malihabadi dussehri mango.

20. Organically produced pokkali rice from Kerala, cooking fuel saving komal chaul from Assam, nannari sharbat from AP, kokam fruit juice from Karnataka and buransh juice from Uttrakhand, low cholestrol malwa potato from MP and natural mineral water from Himalayas are some of examples.
21. Tata Nilgiri tea and Amul alphonso ice cream are the current examples of association of corporate sector with GI, same form of association can be done by the seed companies.
22. For hot pepper, Jamaica has developed a state-of-the-art pest-incidence online traceability system using GIS and GPS technology to ensure that the gall midge and other pests do not become a barrier to North American and European market access. ICT update a current awareness bulletin for ACP agriculture, issue 32, June 2006, CTA, Wageningen.
23. Thomas et al. (2006) through biochemical characterization established that Indian cardamom is different and better than the cardamom from Srilanka and Guatemala.
24. Sea-Buckthorn (*Hippophae rhamnoides*), is a nitrogen fixing shrub found in Ladakh and locally known as '*Tserma*' or '*Jadoo paudha*', the fruits are used to prepare juice. During 1990s, the local women formed a cooperative and started preparing and selling the fruit juice under the name '*Tsetalulu*' in local market. After about ten years, a Delhi based company on the basis of Defence Research and Development Organization (DRDO) refined technology started the production of tetra pack juice under the name of 'Leh Berry'. Now it is an established product in the market. The traditional knowledge of local community formed the basis of commercial application of the technology as refined by a research institute. This product is not registered as GI, similar kind of juice is sold by the China to the tune of Rs 17,000 crore annually. The whole episode raises at least two researchable questions: (i) To what extent benefits have been accrued to the original knowledge holders, and (ii) Can unlimited exploitation of plant lead to loss of species? For details please see an article by Sujatha Padmnabhan (The Hindu, October 4, 2003) and also www.ladakhfoods.com.
25. Kraft Inc., a US company on April 7, 1986 applied the word 'Darjeeling garden' for tea in Unite States Patent and Trademark

Office (USPTO) and got it registered on May 31, 1988 (No. 1490383) and finally USPTO cancelled it on December 5, 1994 under section 8. On July 1, 1988, Tea Board India had applied for certification trademark (CTM) in USPTO for Darjeeling logo for at least 60 percent of tea originating from Darjeeling and got it registered on January 22, 1991 (No. 1632726), renewed in 1997, again renewed on June 30, 2001 for ten years under Section 8. For CTM of word 'Darjeeling' for 100 percent tea originating from Darjeeling, the Tea Board applied in USPTO on January 10, 2002, it was published for opposition on November 19, 2002 and on February 11, 2003 got it registered (No. 2685923). Tea Board in its applications claimed first use on August 31, 1987, first use in commerce on September 10, 1987. The Republic of Tea Inc., a California based company was a licensee of Tea Board to use Darjeeling logo in US. On July 13, 1999 this company applied for registration of 'Darjeeling nouveau' for tea alleging first use on March 1, 1999. Published for opposition on January 4, 2000. On May 1, 2000, Tea Board filed an opposition to the registration of Darjeeling nouveau. Interestingly in this case the applicant tried to defend that 'Darjeeling' is a generic word, therefore CTM given to Tea Board must be cancelled. A telephonic survey was done with 301 of such respondents, who have purchased Darjeeling tea in the previous year of survey, the claims of both the parties were analysed on the basis of 485 responses so received; the applicant and opposer also put the dictionary definitions of claims of each other. But applicant (The Republic of Tea Inc.) failed to show that 'Darjeeling' has a generic meaning. Trademark trial and appeal board of USPTO on January 12, 2006 took the decision to terminate the trademark of Darjeeling nouveau, and finally on November 20, 2006, it was terminated. In February 2000, Tea Board India also put up an opposition for application of 'Divine Darjeeling' for coffee and cocoa in Japan. Despite the long IPR battle, on July 26, 2006 a US company put up an application (Serial No. 76663702) to USPTO for registration of 'Behzad tea or Behzad Darjeeling Tea'. USPTO official document clearly mentions that examination reports find nothing against registering this as a trademark. But on January 3, 2007, USPTO as a form of initial refusal mailed a non-final action because applicant seeks registration of more than one mark in single application, and also applicant has put hand written drawings. For registration of this mark, the non-final action notice should be responded within six months i.e. before June 3, 2007. A French company called Delta Lingerie on March 11, 1997 got registered in USPTO the trademark (No. 2043112) for shirts and ladies wear. It may not be objectionable, as it does not confuse with the tea but as a proactive action Tea Board asked for extension of opposition time twice, it was granted also but nothing much could happen. The trademark is still alive and on March 1, 2007, the company has applied for its renewal for ten years.

26. TAO-TI International Co. Ltd., a Taiwan company filed an application on January 22, 2004 for trademark 'Assam black tea' in USPTO, it was published for opposition on July 5, 2005. On August 3, 2005, Tea Board India asked for extension of period of opposition, it was granted for 90 days ending on November 2, 2005. On the day of expiry of extended time of opposition, Tea Board again asked for extension for 60 more days, it was granted up to January 1, 2006. But by clerical mistake, it was written as January 1, 2005, the trademark was thus inadvertently registered (No. 3034312) on December 27, 2005. Tea Board India further filed an opposition on January 3, 2006; USPTO recognized the procedural failure as trademark can't be registered when opposition phase is still active. On April 25, 2006 applicant filed an abandonment and withdrawal of application, and finally USPTO appeal board cancelled the registration after an inter-partes decision w.e.f. May 18, 2006. This case is unique in itself, and different from 'Darjeeling' in one thing that unlike 'Darjeeling tea', Assam tea is neither registered as GI in India nor as CTM in US, therefore this mark will always be vulnerable for claims by other than genuine owners, and may even create trouble for GI registration in India and further trade to US as a registered GI product.

References

Dev Gangjee (2006): Melton Mowbray and the GI Pie in the Sky: Exploring Cartographies of Protection, *Intellectual Property Quarterly*, No. 3.

Dwijen Rangnekar (2003): The Socio-Economics of Geographical Indications-A Review of Empirical Evidences from Europe, United

Nations Conference on Trade and Development, Geneva.

John McCallum, Meeghan Pither-Joyce, Martin Shaw, Fernand Kenel, Sheree Davis, Ruth Butler, John Scheffer, Jernej Jakse and Michael J. Havey (2007): Genetic Mapping of Sulfur Assimilation Genes Reveals A QTL for Onion Bulb Pungency, *Theoretical and Applied Genetics*, Vol. 114, No. 5.

Latha R. Nair (2006): The Melton Mowbray Pork Pie Case: Lessons for India, *Journal of Intellectual Property Rights*, Vol. 11, May.

Soam, S.K. (2005): Analysis of Prospective Geographical Indications of India, *Journal of World Intellectual Property*, Vol. 8 No. 5.

Swarnim Waglé (2007): *Geographical Indications as Trade-Related Intellectual Property: Relevance and Implications for Human Development in Asia-Pacific,* Discussion paper, Asia-Pacific Trade and Investment Initiative UNDP Regional Centre, Colombo, January.

Thomas, Kizhakkayil, Zachariah, Syamkumar and Sasikumar (2006): Comparative Quality Characterization and Molecular Profiling of Indian, Sri Lankan and Guatemalan Cardamoms, *Food, Agriculture and Environment*, Vol. 4 No. 2.

Index

Index